Frederick Hastings

Obscure characters and minor lights of Scripture

Frederick Hastings

Obscure characters and minor lights of Scripture

ISBN/EAN: 9783337270568

Printed in Europe, USA, Canada, Australia, Japan

Cover: Foto ©Andreas Hilbeck / pixelio.de

More available books at **www.hansebooks.com**

OBSCURE AND MINOR

SCRIPTURE CHARACTERS.

BY

FREDERICK HASTINGS.

LONDON:

THE CHURCH OF ENGLAND BOOK SOCIETY,

11, ADAM STREET, STRAND.

CONTENTS.

CONTENTS.

Obscure Characters.

ANTIPAS; OR, RELIABLE PRINCIPLES.

SCRIPTURE REFERENCE, *Rev.* ii. 13.

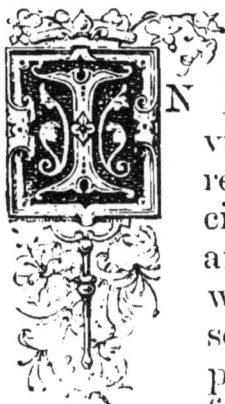

IN Pergamos, a city of Asia Minor, vice, sensuality, and godlessness reigned supreme. It was a very citadel of the prince of darkness, and is called in the chapter from which the text is taken, "Satan's seat." Still Christ had, in such a place, a church, and a band of faithful soldiers who unfurled His banner and battled for His truth. When persecution raged some grew nervous and were frightened into retraction; others held fast to their principles. Among those who were faithful was Antipas. He was a centre of influence, an example of faithfulness, and an inspiration to the fearful. He was a very tower of strength. He acted as the standard-bearer to a small but resolute band of Christians. Against him the efforts of the enemies of the cross were persistently directed. So far from shaking his principles, they were as unsuccessful as are the waves in breaking to pieces some huge boulder over which they dash. They might submerge, but could not shatter. Antipas stood amid the perilous attacks firmly attached to Christ, and when, as a martyr, he died, Christ pronounced over him words of strongest approval, calling him " My faithful martyr." Not only is there divine approval expressed in the words, but also much of affection. In the man of whom the Saviour thus speaks we may find something to interest.

It has been thought by some that the name Antipas is mystical, like "Jezebel," "Balaam," "Egypt," "Sodom," and "Babylon," when they are mentioned in the Apocalypse. It is probably the well-known name of some elder or pastor in the Church at Pergamos, and means, " against all ;" or, " one against many." There is an independent ring about the name. It may have been given to him after death. even as Chrysostom—golden mouth—was given to John. the eloquent preacher of Constantinople.

Most interesting is the study of names and their meanings. There is always some peculiarity or strength of character indicated by a name which has been given, not by parents, but by common consent, as Richard *Cœur de Lion*, or William *the Silent*. If a man inherits a good name he should never stain it, if a common-place name he should make it honourable. Antipas made his to be honoured both on earth and in heaven. Of him we know little. We have just his name and his martyrdom mentioned. The

name agrees with the death. Opposed by all,
he could yet remain faithful to his Lord and to
his principles. We shall, therefore, regard him
as the *impersonation of fealty to principle.*

Antichrist is the name of the one who is
opposed to Christ ; Antipas, here, of him who is
for Christ and opposed to evil. All who have
principles, and act up to them, will find that
they might in a sense claim the name of Antipas.
The world has its principles, practices, maxims,
and objects of pursuit. It tells a man that he
is all right naturally, that he needs no renewal
of heart, and that he is to follow implicitly his
own self-interest. He is to bend and bow, to
truckle or deceive if he can thereby advance his
own welfare. He must not allow himself to be
caught practising deception or the world will
blame him. It will condemn more for the blun-
der of being detected than for the guilt in the
act. Indeed, the world will sometimes speak in
soft tones of a scoundrel if only he has rank, or
wealth, or extreme cleverness ; but it will treat
with unmeasured contempt, weakness, poverty,
or non-success. The principle which the world
recommends is this,—take care of number one,
and trouble not yourself too much about others.
The world believes that it is best rather to take
lessons from the willow than from the oak. The
world resents any introduction of higher principles. It does not, alas, believe in them. But
Christianity introduces higher. It says, "As
ye would that men should do to you, do ye

even so to them." It says. "He that loveth his life shall lose it." It asks, "What shall it profit a man if he shall gain the whole world and lose his own soul?" It insists that we shall not look only on our own things, "but every man also on the things of others," not indeed to covet, but to help. It asserts that we must deny ourselves if we would be followers of Him who laid down His life for us. It breaks down pride, selfishness, and sin, and renews us in the image of our minds. Christianity holds up the mirror of the perfect law of liberty, and makes of those who look therein, "new creatures in Christ Jesus." It binds man to man, and all men to God.

When the principles of Christianity are embraced, they make a man a very Antipas with respect to the world. He will find, ofttimes, things that will clash with conscience, and circumstances such as will demand much casuistical reasoning in the effort to reconcile the claims of God and mammon. Perhaps a man finds that in business he is obliged to look at the worldly saying, "business is business, and religion is religion." He finds that the phrase means that business is a law unto itself, and that religion is not to intrude into its mysteries, or meddle with its maxims. The man wishes to be a true Christian, but he sees that others prosper by following out this maxim, and, perhaps, he is tempted to imitate them. He may know how to palm off the inferior for the good, to make an article possess an attractive appearance when it is almost valueless. Whatever may be his business he may know the special "mysteries" thereof, but he knows that some are such as no man of principle could with a good conscience practise. He has seen, also, at times, some men "fail," "break," or "liqui-date," in order to enrich themselves. They might have prospered had they given due care to business, and avoided habits of extravagance; but they chose to incur debts they could not meet, and then became bankrupt. Now with the man who has unfortunately failed, while doing all he could to succeed, he has the greatest sympathy, and is thankful that there is a way of release provided so that the unfortunate may start afresh ; but where men get the ticket-of-leave from a bankruptcy court, merely to defraud again the confiding, the man of prin-ciple is justly indignant. Not to be able to pay his own lawful debts, would be as the burning stake to him, and he thinks others must share the shrinking. If he cannot pay he will not purchase. He will not pretend to be happy while any are miserable through the loss of amounts he owes. He cannot believe that the law can relieve him from lawful engagements, or that a debt is discharged until it is paid. Being above casuistry, and wishing to live and die with clean hands and a pure heart, he finds that he has, in respect to business, often to follow the example, and imbibe much of the spirit of an Antipas.

It might be even the duty of one employed to act as an Antipas, and rather lose a situation than do that which might be required against conscience. In associating with others also, a man, and especially a young man, may find that he has to be as an Antipas. The conversation of others may be, at times, irreverent and sensual; their habits may be loose; they may seek to allure to drink, dice, or cards; they may draw him into extravagant outlay, and he has to learn to withstand all. He is compelled to associate with them in the factory, shop, or counting-house, but he will not be like them.

There are families also, where, perhaps, there is only one having any spiritual tastes, and the life of that one is a constant rebuke to the worldliness of the rest. That one has there to be a sort of Antipas.

In respect also to social questions there have been those who have had to act as Antipas. The privileged, easy-going, comfortable people, who wish all things to be right, but never lift a finger to bring about that state, are not those who would appreciate his character. Such people would tolerate slavery, injustice, oppression, and wrong, rather than be disturbed themselves or disturb others. The world owes little to such beings; but it owes much to those who seek to remedy evils, and remove wrongs. And yet it will sometimes speak of those who do the most for its benefit as "dangerous persons." The true Antipas, however, will never be troubled at being so

regarded by his fellows, but will be prepared for
any amount of misrepresentation and opposition.
He will remember that, by the reputed religious
people of Christ's day, even the Saviour was regarded as a " Samaritan," as " possessed with a
devil," and as a " blasphemer." The cases are
now very rare in England where a man has to
suffer persecution for the sake of religion. Christianity has gained such power, and so leavened
society with its truths, that greater charity
obtains. There are those holding narrow opinions, who, if they were able, would persecute,
rather than allow others to differ from them ;
but, happily, their beaks are tied, their claws
are cut.

Sometimes in the Church itself there is need
for a man to act as an Antipas. If he finds
non-essentials made the pretext for useless divisions, and cumbersome creeds the means for
lading men's shoulders with burdens grievous to
to be borne, he must speak out. If he finds out
some truth long overlooked, and which it would
be for the welfare of the whole Church to accept,
he may not keep the truth to himself. He may
find himself the subject of much detraction; he
may be condemned as heretical ; but he has to
remember that of others, who have sometimes
been the means of advancing the interests of
truth, many have thus been spoken. The heresy
of one age sometimes becomes the orthodoxy of
the next. Hence truth should be adhered to,
whether it be regarded as heretical or orthodox.

The truth is the only thing about which the man of principle is to be concerned, and his character must be left to take care of itself.

Speaking thus we know that there are many who might, from these remarks, take encouragement to persevere in a course of miserable opposition and crochet-mongering. They might even find excuse for making themselves disagreeable and cross-grained. They might be glad to act the part of Antipas in the Church. One or two such members would be enough, in any Church, to make much unhappiness and bitterness. They might be, like Sanballat and Tobiah, opponents of the welfare of Israel, rather than faithful to Christ like Antipas. Should such go off from a Church it should sing a psalm of thanksgiving. Let them go and associate with those who, like them, are full of crotchets, and it will soon be seen how they will quarrel and separate. Such are false Antipases.

We may always distinguish between the true and the false Antipas. In the Church, or among the sects, are sometimes found those who are stupid, quarrelsome, swordsmen, separatists, people who enjoy a disturbance, who like to create an uproar for the mere excitement of the thing—people who make a great fuss about trifles, pretending they are influenced by principle; these are false Antipases. The true Antipas acts from love, and is tender towards those who bitterly oppose him; thinks not of personal consequences so much as the preserving of conscience. The true often shrinks, trembles, has misgivings, is most anxious to be right, is never boastful, and commits himself and his doings unreservedly to God.

In all his struggles, anxieties, and sufferings, the true Antipas may always be sure of the support of Christ. When the trial comes he finds a strength given such as he little expected. His support is that "hidden manna" of conscious fellowship with the Saviour. He is brought also to understand what Christ had done, and how He had loved, when, single-handed, He struggled in Gethsemane, in the judgment-hall, and on Calvary with unnumbered foes. Suffering for Christ, he is permitted to enter more into the "fellowship of the mystery." But Christ also utters His approval. He speaks of Antipas tenderly as "My faithful martyr." What praise? What an honour to have such mention, by such lips, before men and angels! The sufferings of Antipas must have been terrible, when, by the order of Domitian, he was shut up in the brazen hell, heated red-hot by a large furnace. What, however, was all the pain when Christ was with him and gave such reward? Has Antipas regretted his fealty to principle? Could he speak, he would say, "No; a thousand times, no!"

All who have ever been faithful to Christ, have thus been supported by Him. What but His support could have enabled Paul to withstand those who opposed him, to bear with loneliness, isolation, shipwreck, imprisonment, stripes and browbeatings, cold and hunger, and the keen sword of the executioner? What but this supported an Athanasius when alone he dared to raise a barrier against the Arian heresy on the one hand, and imperial despotism on the other? What but this supported Savonarola under all his cares, and especially at that wonderful moment in the Piazza of Florence, before the great crowds, when, holding aloft the consecrated elements in his hands, his eyes uplifted, and quivering with excitement in his whole aspect, he said, "Lord, if I have not wrought in sincerity of soul, if my word cometh not from Thee, strike me at this moment, and let the fires of Thy wrath enclose me!" What but this conscious presence of Christ, could make a Luther say before a powerful representative of the most tremendous tyranny the world ever knew—that of the papacy—when he refused to recant that which he had written. "Here I stand. I can do no otherwise. God help me?" What but this led Bunyan to say to the judge, "I am at a point with you, and if I were out of prison to-day I would, by the help of God, preach the Gospel to-morrow?" What but this support of Christ, made strong those thirteen martyrs, to whom, recently, that most costly and beautiful terra-cotta monument has been erected in the east of London? Together the thirteen were burned, during the reign of Mary of bloody memory. They said that the Mass is only a profanation of the Lord's Supper; that God was neither spiritually nor corporeally present in the sacrament of the altar; that they were prepared to believe all that could be proved by Holy Scripture; that being condemned to die, they "willingly offered their corrupt bodies to be dissolved in fire." They knew, like Antipas, that they had the support of Christ against a detested idolatry. And the same support and approval we may have if we are faithful to the principles we have conscientiously embraced.

At this day, when there is so much unsettlement as to the principles necessary to be held, and the doctrines essential to salvation, it is of the highest importance to foster this spirit of fealty to Christ. The world likes Christ no better than ever, but there are more Christians than ever to moderate its spleen. The truth of Christ is not more acceptable to the world it condemns, but the world now does not attempt to repress truth by force. It rather seeks to kill it, by giving it open countenance but secret enmity. Almost as much grace on the part of a Christian is needful to live consistently in the midst of the present subtile temptations of a smooth prosperity, as to go to prison or to the stake. When the storm is raging, the captain's watchful eye and sailor's ready help may keep the ship from wreckage, but what can they do against the calm and heat of the tropics? Strong winds, while they bring risk, also drive

onward the ship to her destination; but the
calm and heat may so enervate the crew, or
foster disease that—as in cases we have known
—not a man has been left unstricken by fever,
or able to stand at the wheel. Thus it was
more easy to be faithful and watchful in times
of persecution such as overtook Antipas, than it
is in these times of tolerance and prosperity.
When a man is likely to suffer severely for his
opinions he is sure to be careful as to what
principles he embraces. Still, all should be as
concerned to be right and to hold the truth
whether they have to suffer or not for their
opinions.

Now there are several points on which we
are bound to have settled convictions if we wish
to obtain the salvation of the soul. We are told
in God's Word concerning the person and work of
Christ, "neither is there salvation in any other."
Christ is the only hope of our race, and the only
Saviour of the soul. "No man cometh unto the
Father but by Me," said Christ. These words
are not a mere exaggerated utterance, but a
merciful limitation and direction. We know
what we have to do, and to whom only we
must go. We know who has the special and
righteous claim to our service and love. Christ
invites men in tenderest terms to follow Him.
We know how He wept over those who would
not receive Him. He wept because He knew
the consequences of that rejection. Similar
bitter consequences, now as then, follow neglect

and rejection. We must, therefore, decide this, as to whether the principle of our lives shall be devotion to Christ, or neglect. The whole character of the future must depend on that. If we love Him, we shall seek to serve Him in every way; by controlling sin in the soul, and striving to lessen the sin and misery in the world.

But some have not had the courage, even in this land of Bibles and sanctuaries, to confess Christ. They are waiting to follow others, but dare not lead. Various are the excuses they make, but the real reason is the non-possession of faith like that of the martyr of Pergamos. Let them have that, and then like him they could stand against all. Let them have that, and who can tell what deeds of valour they might not perform for Christ. They would be ready, like Antipas, to die rather than know that His cause had been disgraced, or His standard lowered.

In a terrible conflict in Virginia, a young soldier of the federal army, who was the best man of his regiment, was wounded. He was just passing a ball into his gun, when a shot passed through his left hip and shattered it. He fell, but his captain lifted him up again, and carried him to a place of temporary safety, the young soldier protesting, "Never mind me, captain, but don't let that flag go down!" His one thought was not of himself, but of the honour of his country and flag. And that should be the thought and utterance of any of us with respect to Christ and His truth— "Never mind me, but don't let that flag go down." If we have to suffer, to resist, to wrestle "unto blood," striving against sin; if we have to bear with scorn or contumely, with hatred and persecution, let each one say, "Never mind me, but don't let His flag go down!" If that should be the aim of our life, if fealty to Christ and to principle characterize us, we may be assured that He will not let us go unrewarded, but will say of us, with the same tenderness of approval he gave to Antipas, "Well done, good and faithful servants; enter ye into the joy of your Lord." As He said to the Church at Pergamos, He now says to you, "To him that overcometh will I give to eat of the hidden manna, and will give him a white stone, and in the stone a new name written, which no man knoweth saving he that receiveth it." Amen.

SCRIPTURE REFERENCE. *Acts* xiii. 1.

SOMEWHERE about the time that Christ was born, two men, whose names are here mentioned in close conjunction, came into existence. Herod Antipas was born in the purple, Manaen in homespun. The first was the son of a king, the latter of some plebeian. Herod the Great had a son named Antipas, who, either on account of the indifference of his mother or of her absorption in court duties, or on account of the need of the child for a healthier training than could be given to him in the palace, was sent out, as a mere infant, to be brought up by a stranger.

In an unknown village lived a woman who had a son, named Manaen, whom she tenderly nourished. To her was committed the care of Herod Antipas. We know not how she came to be selected for what would at that time, doubtless, be thought a great honour. It has been surmised that it was owing to her being the wife of one of whom Josephus speaks. He narrates the story, that one day, when Herod the Great was a mere youth and on his way to school, a man, named Menahen, who was an Essene,—one of an earnest religious order in Judæa,—met him and foretold that he would one day be king of the Jews. The prognostication seemed then unlikely to be fulfilled; but afterwards when the prophecy was verified, and Herod was firmly seated on the throne, he is said to have highly honoured Menahen. It would appear quite possible and probable that to this man's wife, having a son named after his father, the first Herod committed the care of his son Antipas.

On the slope of some hill, or on the marge of some river or lake, two boys might, centuries ago, have been seen playing together. They, doubtless, amused themselves, as children of all ages have done, by the simplest means. A few stones or sticks served to interest them. They may have laid out shell gardens, or designed sand castles, or set afloat boats of papyrus or of reeds. Together they played, ate, and slept. A wanderer looking upon them would have thought them equals. They were treated as such, although one was a poor man's son and the other a prince.

Now, here are two boys starting together in life, but what different careers will be theirs. Their lives illustrate the diverse destinies of the children in our homes and schools.

Let us follow a little further in life the two whose names are here mentioned. Antipas and Manaen are no longer youths. They have had to separate, possibly with deep regret on both sides. It is said that the love of foster-brothers is oft beyond that of actual brothers. Manaen may not have known, until the parting, that his supposed brother was a prince of the reigning house. This may have explained to him certain greater indulgences allowed his foster-brother, indulgences which may have sometimes caused Manaen a little jealousy. They part. Herod goes to dwell in a palace, to be further subjected to Grecian and Roman culture, and trained in the graces of courtly life ; Manaen remains to toil with his father in obscurity. learning, as best he may, how to be content. and catching at any hint that his father may drop concerning the coming of the Messiah, the hope of Israel.

Let us follow them further still. Herod the Great is dead, and in the partition of his dominion, Herod Antipas is called to rule as Tetrarch over the province of Galilee. He has certainly in this position enough adulation from fawning flatterers to disturb the balance of his brain, and every opportunity for the gratification of pride, ambition, and lust. He soon allows his self-indulgent nature to be seen. He becomes the slave of his passions, and even enters into an incestuous marriage with Herodias, the wife of his brother Philip. He yields to the whims of the hour, and because at one time pleased with the graceful dancing of the daughter of Herodias, promises her largess, even to the half of his kingdom. He gives utterance to a foolish, rash oath, involving fearful consequences to others, and even when he perceives the dreadful results of his oath, does not withdraw from his false position. Rather than confess a mistake, he will sacrifice a prophet. The man he slew was one who had led him to do many good deeds, one whom he knew to be the most honest man in his kingdom, one who was the last of the prophets and the immediate herald of Christ. Herod the Great had in vain tried to slay Jesus in infancy, but his son Antipas succeeded in slaying the fore-runner of the Messiah.

Antipas had his seasons of self-condemnation and of bitter longings. He had 'heard John gladly' in many things. He had even wished to see Christ. He had some faith also in the unseen world. He was superstitious, and be-lieved, shortly after the death of John, that the Baptist had come to life again in the person of Jesus, and that, therefore, 'mighty works' showed themselves forth in him. His faith was merely a faith of fear. When he wished to see Christ, it was only that he might be gratified by beholding some marvellous work, or that he might gain over His tremendous powers to his own interest. Christ, who knew his foxlike nature, would not con-descend to be a marvel-worker. Herod, with his men of war, even mocked at Christ. He insulted the Saviour with a sham dignity in the purple robe with which he caused Christ to be clothed and sent back to Pilate.

Herod had an evil genius—a subtle woman. Herodias persuaded him to try to be King in Galilee, instead of Tetrarch. Not content with being a mere viceroy, he desired to be a sort of khedive. In carrying out his ambitious designs he went to Rome, where, instead of being advanced by his suzerain, he was met by accusations of certain crimes he could not deny. The court condemned him, and he was not permitted quietly to resign and enjoy a large allowance from the Roman civil list, but was banished by the Emperor Caligula to Lyons. Here he ended his days in poverty and disgrace. What a reverse for one who had tasted the sweets of royal power! In banishment he died, forsaken by man and by God. A life of promise and power was quenched in frustrated hopes, in misery and despair. His banishment, disappointment, and despair, were only typical of those fearful consequences which, in the life which succeeds this, follow all wrong-doing. We shrink from the endurance of such consequences ourselves, and tremble at the thought that our dear ones may be exposed by their own heedlessness and sin to similar woe.

Let us turn now to the life of Manaen. Perhaps, favoured by Herod, he rose to some position of vantage. That which we know with certainty of him is, that he was at Antioch, and that he became eminent in the infant Church planted in that city. He was a prophet and teacher—the noblest of all callings. He had somehow been brought to believe in Jesus of Nazareth, and to consecrate to Him the best energies of life. His training, by pious if humble parents, may have prepared him to receive impressions from any godly man with whom he might in after life come in contact. Doubtless, he had a good mother. Nearly all the good in any man is traceable to a pious mother. A gentleman, whose mother died while he was yet young, has spoken of the influence that godly woman had on his whole life. He could never forget how she, with her hand on his head, first taught him to say the Lord's prayer. Whenever he felt tempted to do any wrong, the pressure of that hand seemed always present, and he dared not yield to temptation. "How can I commit this wickedness," he thought, "and sin not only against God, but against my mother?" Would that every boy had such memories of his mother!

It is well to keep sons and daughters as long as possible under home influence. Very common is the practice, at this day, of bringing up children by proxy. They are often sent away to distant schools to be trained amid a mass of others, and in this mass may be some with whom, if parents knew their character, they would shudder to think of their dear ones being associated. Parents run great risks in thus bringing up their children by proxy. Who can care for children like their own parents? Manaen's mother could take a Herod to nurse, to board, and to train ; but a Herod does not become a Manaen.

Doubtless, there were in Manaen inherited qualities of goodness that made a great difference. Moral qualities, as well as mental, can be transmitted. We know that some children seem to have from their birth a great love of goodness and truth. They grow up, and when under the power of the Holy Spirit they are brought to love Christ, and to see that they need renewal and cleansing from sin, their lives become more beautiful still. They also become more useful, because goodness becomes a fixed habit and not a fitful sentiment. Manaen must have owed much to his parents for an inherited love of truth and for a power of will which led him, on seeing what was right and true, to decide, and abide by it. When he came to know Him who was "the Way, the Truth, and the Life," he instinctively and for ever became attached to Him.

Perhaps when Manaen thought of joining the disciples of Christ, worldly considerations, averse to such action, would present themselves. Must he sacrifice the interest which the great Herod takes in him? Shall he, the foster-brother of a prince, become an associate of a despised Nazarene? Whatever sacrifices or risks were involved, they were cheerfully faced. Acting with decision, Manaen enrolled himself under the banner of Christ, and so faithfully served Him that he came to take rank with a Paul, and to be trusted by the whole Church.

Manaen had reason for great thankfulness that God had, probably, not only given him godly parents, but that He had also given him grace in his heart. This led him to shun evil and speak the truth. We know not the rule by which God acts, but we are sure that there is no arbitrariness in the methods of the bestowal of the Holy Spirit. The Great Father is devoted to the well-being of all, and there is not a child living with whom His Spirit is not striving to lead it into the way of life.

Manaen had also to thank God that he had seen the beauty of the doctrine of Christ, the glory of His grace, and that He had given him a work to do. He preached Christ's Gospel, visited from house to house, and sought in every way to win souls to newness of life. He is supposed to have been one of the seventy apostles sent out at one time by Christ. If so, he had enjoyed the high privilege of knowing Jesus personally. Anyhow, he became a worker in Christ's vineyard, a soldier in the Redeemer's army, and a king and priest unto God.

The world, looking on the lives of Manaen and Herod, would probably pronounce that of the latter the more brilliant, but certainly Manaen's was the more valuable. The world could better have spared its tetrarchs and monarchs than its teachers and prophets. The former have often only thrown back the best interests of their fellows, especially when they have played the dreadful game of war, while the latter always advanced men to higher levels, to love of peace, increase of charity, and the lessening of sorrow.

Doubtless, Manaen's end was peace. Dying steadfast in the faith, he would afterwards be received with warm welcome into the presence of His God and Saviour. Standing at the judgment bar of God, as Herod had stood at that of Cæsar, he would find no one to accuse him ; but if Sin or Satan rose, he could cry, "Who is he that condemneth ? It is Christ that died." Not disgrace and banishment, but blessedness and Divine approval are his for aye. Eternity opens for him with a glow as of a summer's morning, while the ending of Herod's life was lit up only with the lurid glare of stormy terrors.

To what a distance were the foster-brothers removed by death! No line would ever be long enough to measure the distance separating them ; no plummet heavy enough to sound the depths of the woe of the one, or the happiness of the other. How different were their destinies ! And such may be the diverse destinies of some of those young people who sit together, who are taught in the same school, and perhaps even by the same teacher. Such also may be the diverse destinies of some in the same family, loved equally by their parents. What gulfs may widen between that son and daughter of yours ! You love them both with all the intensity of your nature, and can you bear to contemplate the possible difference in their destinies ? Oh, should there be any chance of saving any from such loss as is involved in living and dying without an interest in Christ, ought we not to do all we can to effect their salvation? We ought to act as if all depended on us. We ought carefully to watch every tendency in the nature, and to seize every opportunity of giving a right bias, so that they may become Christian Manaens, and not Christless Herods.

ADONI-BEZEK;

OR, RIGHTEOUS RETRIBUTION.

SCRIPTURE REFERENCE, *Judges* i. 7.

MANY men in all ages have taken a certain delight in seeing others suffer. They have racked their brains to devise some more exquisite mode of torturing others. Great has been the ingenuity exercised in the invention of instruments of torture. Burning without blistering, stretching without killing have been arts. In the accompaniments of *war*, not only have the most terrible injuries been inflicted during the battle itself, but when the fight is over, the persons of the conquered have sometimes been subjected to worse torments than any they could have endured on the field. These doings have often been defended on the ground that they were necessary to self-defence and self-preservation. Alas, they are sometimes only to be explained by the depraved desire in the human heart of exercising arbitrary and cruel power. The practice referred to in this chapter—that of excision of the thumbs of captives—comes under this class. It may have been defended because it disabled from handling the sword and from running from the pursuers. Dread device and dastardly defence!

It was the practice in Rome to exempt all men who had lost their thumbs from serving in the army. Sometimes this exemption was abused. The Senate once condemned Caius Valienus to perpetual imprisonment because he had cut off the thumb of his left hand, in order to excuse himself from going on a certain expedition. Indeed, our English word *poltroon*, coward, is derived from the Italian [poltrone] signifying "a man with his thumbs cut off." Probably it was to brand men as cowards that Adoni-bezek carried on such a cruel practice. This method of branding afforded a certain malign gratification to those who had the power thus to punish others, while it did something towards crippling the power of revolt.

The excision must have been performed in a particular way—which would be most painful—otherwise death would have speedily ensued. Doubtless many would, even with this precaution, die from the infliction. It seems, however, to have afforded amusement to those who were onlookers. It is strange how men can behold such things without, mentally, placing themselves in the position of those compelled to submit to such cruelty. But men get, by *education*, gradually accustomed to such sights. Frequently the process of education in evil begins very early. A child forms the habit of tormenting insects and mute creatures. That is the preparatory process. Doubtless the education of Adoni-bezek began early. Certainly if he had others to help him, he was an apt pupil. He had evidently delighted in practising as much cruelty as possible. It had been his boast at one time, that so many kings had not only suffered by excision of their thumbs, but had been reduced also to the position of dogs. "To gather meat under a table," was the proverbial expression for such a position. If he had thus treated seventy-two kings, it is probable that he had maltreated, or caused to be tormented, many others of inferior rank.

But the victorious Israelites advance, and Adoni-bezek has to fight a battle in which, instead of being the victor, he is the vanquished. He is taken and led, a prisoner, into the presence of his conqueror. Never had he anticipated this; much less that he himself would have to suffer as others had done through him. The Israelites knew of this horrible practice. It had been a matter of common report how cruelly he treated the vanquished. To punish him, they inflict the same penalty. With hands and feet writhing from the recent excision, he makes this acknowledgment: "As I have done, so God hath requited me."

Adoni-bezek notices the remarkable *correspondence between previous barbarity and present suffering.* When men suffer, they look back and

ask themselves why such a trial has come upon
them—what action of their own has caused it?
Men are never willing *at first* to blame themselves
for any evil that may befall them. But the nature of the punishment in this case compels
Adoni-bezek to trace his suffering to his own
act. Had he suffered from a wound in battle, or
fallen as he led his army, or had he been simply
imprisoned, or had his eyes been put out, as
were those of one of the kings of Judah, he
would not so readily have connected his misfortune with his previous wrongdoings. There
is, however, in his sufferings something so
forcibly recalling his own misdeeds, that he
himself calls his torture a requital. He sees a
similarity between his own sin and that which
had fallen upon him. He takes it in the sense
of retribution. Why? Because conscience told
him he had done evil.

It is a very unwarrantable notion to think
that because trouble overtakes a man, therefore
he must have done something wrong proportion-
ate to the evil. A man may be overtaken by an
accident, but he may for all that be a good man.
Christ rebuked this erroneous notion when he
spoke of those upon whom the tower of Siloam
fell, as not being sinful above all others. Paul
suffered shipwreck, and the Melitans, slaves to
a similar superstition, when they saw the viper
come out of the fire, said among themselves,
"This man is a murderer." He was no murderer, however, and they soon changed their

minds. Indeed, the noblest ofttimes have to
suffer, while the most unworthy escape. How
many have fallen victims to the anger of those
who have had vested interests in some giant
wrong, while the oppressors of the poor
wretches they sought to liberate, live on in
courtly luxury. Suffering may be sacrifice or
discipline, not necessarily retribution.

If great suffering in this world always implied
great sin committed by the sufferer, then Christ
must have sinned. If we think thus, and had
been at Jerusalem when Christ was crucified,
we should probably have joined with the chief
priests in mocking and vexing His soul. We
know, however, that in Him was no sin, and
we ascribe His suffering to His love of the
oppressed. This made it sacrifice.

The evil which falls upon us may often be
the *consequence of the wrongdoing of others.*
When the captain of a vessel spends his time
in dissipation, drinking and card-playing with
two or three passengers, neglecting all care
about the vessel,—should she founder, the innocent go down with the guilty. We should
not in that case say that all were guilty because
they had been involved in the same catastrophe.
The disaster, which to some might be but the
beginning of a death that never dies, might be
to others the commencement of a life of bliss
that knows no end.

We need not then see in every misfortune a
token of God's displeasure. God does not oc-

cupy Himself in tracking always the wrongdoer from place to place, until He finally brings him to punishment in this life. *Sometimes,* however, various circumstances connected with bringing the offender to justice are so remarkable, and seemingly so responsive to the crime, that there naturally arises in the minds of others the belief that his misfortune is a special and divinely imposed retribution.

Retribution may be the *working out of certain natural laws.* Nature in such cases works in harmony with the spiritual world, executing judgment from without. Generally the punishment is from within, by the conscience, and in a natural way. It was the *conscience* of Adonibezek which led him thus to tremble at what he understood as the consequence of his own sin. Had he suffered the same treatment, never having injured others in the same way, it is not probable that he would have seen in it a requital of his own sin. That he should so see it, shows that when he had thus cruelly used the seventy-two kings one after the other, the voice of conscience had protested against it. It had been for some long time silent. Now, however, its power returns, and with fearfully startling emphasis asserts, "Thou didst this to others, now it comes upon thyself. Thou didst mock at the calamity of others, now it comes upon thee, and thou shrinkest." He sees that he had acted proudly and wantonly. He has to suffer, but it would be far more easy to bear his sufferings if conscience would not so bitterly remind him of the correspondence between previous performances and present pains.

The recognition of the correspondence between past acts and his present misfortune *leads Adoni-bezek to ascribe it to a Divine hand.* "*God* has requited me." He was not an Israelite, but was probably an idolater, and he may have trusted in false gods for a long time. He had ascribed to their power his success in previous campaigns, but at last, finding himself beaten, he acknowledges the superior power of the God of the Israelites. It was a dread of that God which compelled the confession. He had heard of God, and what he had done to other nations; now he finds himself conquered, and is led to attribute his personal sufferings to the God of the Israelites. The God of Israel was known as a holy and just God. Hence he tacitly recognises the *justice* of the punishment which had fallen upon him. It is a righteous and divine requital.

God has so arranged natural law that it works in harmony with eternal justice. There is a subtle connection between our acts and our sufferings. We may see illustrations of this every day. A man may act in a certain loose and careless way and prepare for himself consequences the most terrible and unlooked for. Another gives way to fierce and ungoverned passions, and makes himself, thereby, wretched. Another chooses to spend his time only in the pursuits of pleasure, and to squander his money

on every foolish thing that pleases his eye;
he soon finds himself without either the power
to enjoy, or the money to procure enjoyment.
Another gives way to pilfering, and soon finds
himself discharged, characterless.   Even if he
is not punished by law, he is dishonoured.   Or
a youth may have kind parents, and every opportunity of making his way in the world, but
he gives way to dissipated habits, and finally,
when character is gone and friends are dead, is
glad to earn the most trifling sum under men
whom he once despised.   A just retribution
in all such cases certainly follows the sin.   Like
Adoni-bezek, such must confess that "God hath
requited" the wrong-doing.

This Law works silently, tardily, but surely.
See that tree standing amidst many others.   It
spreads its branches wide.   Its dark green
foliage is as thick, its beauty as great, as that
of others.   Year after year has it stood firm.
Many a storm has howled through its numberless branches and threatened to uproot it.   Many
trees around have fallen, but that tree still stands.
You say, "It will stand for ever!"   One night,
however, a storm, less severe perhaps than many
that have preceded it, sweeps over the land.
The morning breaks, and men look out to see the
damage done, and the very tree that seemed as
though it would stand for ever, is the only one
fallen.   How is this?   Some slight gash with a
knife when it was a sapling, just above some
branch, has let the rain soak in.   Gradually the

heart rotted out, and a mere shell of bark has been left. The appearance was good, but it had no solidity. Hence its fall. Thus with many whose sin is prolonged and whose punishment seems delayed. It will come by and by. Then, writhing under the bitter consequences, the transgressor is compelled to say, "As I have done, so God hath requited me."

This acknowledgment concerning the just requital of sin, is *sure to take place in the other world, if not in this.*

We shall there see that each punishment is natural, that God does not go out of His way to punish, but that it grows out of our sin. It is not an arbitrary appointment. Death has been aforetime the appointed penalty for stealing. That was not a natural, but an arbitrary consequence. Man appointed it. Death following upon the wilful leap from a lofty precipice, is a natural consequence. All will see clearly, hereafter, that ruin is the natural effect of folly. We have thrown ourselves from a high vocation into the deep abyss of sin, and if without Divine help, must perish.

Pagan mythology taught that the mean and sly will, in the other world, take the lynx form; the slanderers, that of the vampire fanning ever to sleep, and sucking the life-blood at the same time; that the hypocritical will be as crocodiles, crawling in the mud and shedding false tears; and that the narrow and bigoted, fearful of truth and loving error, may be as owls, hooting amid darkness and ruin, in the forsaken and desolate regions of the other world.

May not the dishonest man there have to cringe and hide himself still more? May not the drunken man have a constant craving, a burning thirst, a racking brain? May not the ambitious man have a constant anxiety to obtain power, and the torment of always being supplanted, or effectually checked, by others? May not the avaricious man be in a constant fever of suspicion? May not the ill-tempered man be in a constant whirl of passion, and make himself more and more wretched? May not the ruthless and cruel fear the scorn of their victims and clutches of their enemies? May not the voluptuary have to bear the torment of an inflamed heart and ungratified lusts? There is a frightful force in the Saviour's figure of "the worm that never dieth, and the fire that shall never be quenched." Every hasty word, every evil thought, every malicious action, every wilful neglect, will receive its appropriate retribution. God hath established the unswerving law that "whatsoever a man soweth, that shall he also reap." Even an idolatrous Adoni-bezek saw the correspondence between past cruelty and present anguish; and confessed the justice of the requital in the remarkable words, "As I have done, so God hath requited me."

MNASON, THE AGED CYPRIOT.

SCRIPTURE REFERENCE—*Acts* xxi. 16.

ON his last journey to Jerusalem, Paul was accompanied by certain disciples from Cæsarea. These seem to have introduced another disciple to St. Paul, an aged man, named Mnason; and concerning him there is a tradition that he was one of the seventy disciples whom, in addition to the twelve apostles, Jesus had sent forth. This man appears to have accompanied Paul to Jerusalem, and to have afforded, as he had a house of his own in Jerusalem, shelter and hospitality to the apostle to the Gentiles. Mnason was a Cypriot by birth, but he may have been a Jew by extraction. We know not whether his parents were natives of Cyprus or whether they were simply Jewish colonists, but if the former then Mnason doubtless became a proselyte to Judaism first and an adherent of Christianity afterwards. Anyhow we are told that he was an old disciple, not in the sense of having been converted late in life, but a disciple of long standing, an *early* disciple, as the revised version has it, one who had long served Jesus. If the tradition mentioned be reliable then he would have known Jesus in the flesh and have had instruction from Him, and in this would have an advantage over the one whom he now invited to be his guest when at Jerusalem.

As we look at Mnason we get a hint how with *increasing years should come an increasing delight in learning of Christ.* Mnason was a disciple still. There was much for him yet to learn. Perhaps he was eager to meet Paul that he might hear from him not only much concerning the dealings of Christ with him, but the revelations of Christ to him. There would also be many passages in sacred writ, in the old prophets relating to Christ, on which he would be glad to have light, and he may have sought this introduction to Paul and offered him the use of his home in Jerusalem that he might have opportunity for uninterrupted enquiry and research. The very meaning of his name is suggestive in this light, for it may be interpreted as "diligent seeker," "exhorter," or "one who remembers," a true disciple. To love the new and attractive is natural. Familiarity oft wears away the charm of that which was once most absorbing. Those who begin early to run with alacrity the way of peace often slacken their pace as the journey lengthens. Here, however, is one who began early in life to serve Christ, and whose love to Him remained fresh and fervent

and fragrant during all that long interval between His ascension to heaven and the going
up of Paul for the last time to Jerusalem.
Time is the test of true piety. Not all who
" gird on the harness " take it off with honour.
But Mnason could take off his with honour, for
he bore the honourable title of " an old
disciple." He had not let the mainspring of
devotion run down. No backslider was he,
keeping the face heavenwards but slipping daily
further away from the abode of eternal rest.
Though many years faithful, his piety was only
the more intense as the time for the fuller and
permanent vision of the Saviour drew near.

Now there should be in every aged believer
this firm, growing faith, and the conviction of
Christ's preciousness. This should be the pro-
duct of experience of His constant presence,
power, and sympathy. Alas, some live only on
a past experience. They hope that on account
of a feeling of devotion experienced or act of
consecration performed at some past period of
life, acceptance with Christ is theirs, but there
has been no attainment of that " full assurance
of faith" on which the apostle Paul laid such
strong emphasis. They have been justified by
faith, but have not passed far on from the entrance to Christianity. Their aspect is rather
that of pardoned criminals than of beloved children. They have not seen how God not only
blots out sin but lavishes His love and grace
daily upon them. They live hoping in His mercy,

but not rejoicing in His love. With Mnason
there appears, from the brief mention of him and
the manner of it, reason to infer that he was
not a mere hanger-on to the skirts of Christianity, but that he was known as a disciple ripe
in knowledge, in spiritual experience, in fervency
of spirit and in devotion to his Master, his
Saviour and God.

Again, we see in this "old disciple" a hint
that *with added years should come increasing
desire to be helpful to others.* Readily Mnason
seems to have placed his house at the disposal of
Paul. Not only so, but even though so far advanced in years he undertakes a long and wearisome journey, glad to be permitted to minister to the wants and cheer the spirit of
one who had so diligently served his Master,
and who had received such signal blessing from
Him. There was evidently, by the way in
which he is mentioned, none of the spirit of
regret and complaint that sometimes makes the
presence of the aged annoying to the younger.
He was not always looking for help from others,
but considering how he might best be helpful to
others. And this spirit would make advancing
years a joy. He would live to do good, and
when the field of his life was covered with good
deeds like a harvest of golden-hued corn, the
shocks would be garnered, and the sheaves
brought in with many a shout of rejoicing. It
is one of the promises of the Holy Word "Those
that be planted in the house of the Lord shall

flourish in the courts of our God. They shall still bring forth fruit in old age; they shall be fat and flourishing" (Ps. xcii. 14). It was not an honour without risk that Mnason gained by offering to extend hospitality to Paul when he should reach Jerusalem. He was, however, willing to share the apostle's danger, and as a true disciple would not count his life dear to him in the service of Christ. This aged disciple was willing, therefore, to sacrifice self if he might only be helpful to another. Many are ready to help when it costs nothing but words, or so much coin, but when it means personal effort and possible personal inconvenience in obliging, greater hesitancy is manifested. Generous, helpful old men like Mnason teach such timid souls a lesson. Happy that Association or Church that has among its adherents such men—helpful spirits!

How Paul must have been cheered in his great work by the wise counsels and loving words of Mnason! How he would thank God for the happy circumstance that led him into connection with this old disciple! And thus, many a pastor and missionary has to thank God for the aged helper. Sometimes the aged are not of a helpful spirit. Sometimes they complain of the present and praise the past—see nothing but evil, ruin, and disaster in the one; and prosperity, purity, and perfection in the other. "The former days were better than these," is their constant cry. They would say the same concerning this age fifty years hence, could they live as long. They have a depressing instead of a helpful influence. Their breath is that of the east wind. They are not helpful as Mnason; and if such had met with Paul, instead of offering a home to the great missionary, they would have been ready to dissuade with such energy, that Paul would say, with increased emphasis, "What mean ye to weep and to break my heart?"

Some men become aged, and yet have seen very little of life. Such may retain a calm and hopeful spirit, because of their inexperience of the ways of the world. But where men see much of life it is a very great temptation to grow hard, narrow, severe, believing good only of the early portion of life, and evil of the latter. Where this temptation is overcome, and men grow simple, sunny-hearted, trustful, hopeful, more devout as they grow older; where they are loved more for what they are than for what they do, where they retain the heart of a child, or gain such goodness that their heart is like a full honeycomb, there is a charm about them inexpressible, and an influence flowing from them incalculable in its worth. To look at them is "as when you watch the mountain-tops, where snows lie thick above you; while you sit among the vines and roses in quiet nooks, and hear the birds singing in the copse summer songs." Such must have been the sight of Mnason when he first met Paul;

or of Simeon in the temple, holding in his arms
the infant Jesus; or of John the apostle, when
at Ephesus he taught the assembly of strong
men to be as little children, loving one another;
or such an one as Paul the aged, showing the
stern men of Rome how to face death unflinch-
ingly, because in him was the gentle life and
faith unwavering in the Christ who died for him.

Again, in such lives as those of Mnason we
see *hints of immortality.* It is a great thing
when men have so lived that time shall have
done all it can for them. We feel that such
lives as these cannot be brought up to a certain
point of perfection only to be cast aside as
rubbish. What! shall time have done so much
towards fitting them for an eternity, and yet eternity never be theirs? Shall a man gain a life-long
experience, a ripe age, a longing for, as well as fitness for immortality, and immortality never be
his? Would a watch-maker make a clock, ornate
and elaborate as that at Berne or Strasbourg, only
to break it up; or would he intend it to run
down like that at Versailles, which stopped at
the moment of a monarch's death, and has never
been wound up again? Is the sun to be surrounded by so much of amber and purple glory
in the setting, but to know no morrow's rising?
Are those who have cherished high ideals, who
have striven hard to attain them, but have
felt that still there was something richer beyond, never to have the innate longing satisfied?
They cannot if there be no immortality. We

believe that such as Mnason come to the grave as shocks of corn fully ripe, and that the seed of the shocks will afterwards be sure to give a larger, richer harvest in eternity. A good old age is suggestive of the certainty of immortality.

In some men who are aged, the results seem unworthy of the length of life. Days have come and gone, like the tides that ebb and flow; and there has been no such change in the aspect of their nature as could even be found on the face of a hard, water-worn rock. This, alas, is painful. Life with such is as spoiled canvas, as Sèvres china so broken that it cannot be mended, or a blotted volume which has no meaning even when deciphered.

Some long lives are anything but beautiful, although interesting; and some are injurious, misleading, and false, like the notorious sheep-skin manuscript of Deuteronomy. There was in that the appearance of worth, the promise of fresh light on holy writ, when its blackened surface and almost illegible letters should have yielded up their meaning—but it was a forgery. Some old men are very difficult to understand; and when they are understood, are like that manuscript—a sham and a forgery. They have taken the blessings of God for many years, and have had all the benefit of experience; but there is no glory given back to God, and no fitness for the presence of God or entrance, by faith in Christ, on a blissful im-

mortality. They may be, as alas some aged men
are, not old disciples, like Mnason; but only
aged sinners. Terrible sight! woeful state!
God save us all from drifting on to such a state!
It is a dreary state, like a misty, bitterly
cold region, with no sunshine breaking through
upon it. One minister said he had been twenty
years a preacher, but had known few conversions
after fifty; and Dean Swift said, in his usual cau-
stic way, "When men grow virtuous in old age
they are merely making a sacrifice to God of
the devil's leavings." Still let us come, even
though we come late. If any who have lived long
cannot be old disciples in the sense of being long
established, they may be in the sense that they
are aged in penitence, and strong in love to
Him who has borne with the mistakes,
wrongs, and neglects of an extended life.
They may, as the bard of Avon expresses
it, "begin to patch up the poor body for
heaven."

Oh, it is pitiable to see an old man without
religion. He loses two worlds at once—that
which is behind, and that which is beyond.
One has said truly that there is "no more
repulsive spectacle than that of an old man
who will not forsake the world which has
already forsaken him." Of all the unwise, he
is the most to be blamed. Grey-headed folly
is the crown of folly. Let us so live that the
good results shall be commensurate with length
of life. Let us so live, that we may say—as

the venerable and devout Countess of Hun-
tingdon said in her eighty-fourth year,—"I am
old, my work is done, I have nothing now to
do but to go to my Father." Let us live so
that when we come to the mountain-top of
life, we may look back, if with a great sense
of unworthiness through sin, at least with some
satisfaction through the power of Christ in us.
Let us so live that at last the shadow of the
cross, and not the burden of sin, may fall over
us. Let us so live that we may be like Mnason,
helpful and hopeful in old age; and suggestive
in the glory of our life of the promise of a rich
immortality. Let us so live that we may not
find ourselves at the end like that sinning
monarch who had in his dreariness to confess—

> " My way of life
> Is fallen into the sere, the yellow leaf :
> And that which should accompany old age,
> As honour, love, obedience, troops of friends,
> I must not look to have ; but in their stead
> Curses not loud, but deep, mouth-honor breath,
> Which the poor heart would fain deny, and dare not."

Let us so live that when we go, others shall
regret, and not rejoice, over our departure.
Let us so live that, like "ripe fruit we shall
drop into our mother's lap, or be with ease
gathered, not harshly plucked for death." So
let us live, that after much tossing on life's
rough sea, we may come to the bright harbour at last. So let us live, that at the end

of life, the partition between us and the glory
land shall have become so thin and shattered,
that a single touch shall at once cast it down
and leave us, as young or old disciples,
standing in the flood of light that comes from
Him who sitteth upon the throne,—from Him
whose majesty and whose glory filleth heaven.
Let us so live, that when the silver cord is
loosed and the golden bowl broken, the
pitcher broken at the fountain, or the wheel
at the cistern, "the dust shall return to
the earth as it was; and the spirit unto God
who gave it."

THE PRINCE OF MESHECH; OR, THOUGHT AND STERLING CHARACTER.

SCRIPTURE REFERENCES—*Ezekiel* xxxviii. 10 *and Proverbs* xxiii. 7.

HE prophecy of this chapter has reference to some people dwelling in the remote North, who were opposed to the Israel of God. Some have thought that the Scythians are referred to, and that as they and other invaders were opposed to the people of God, they were to be overthrown. There is much mystery about the land and around the Prince of Meshech. Anyhow, there was much terror spread by him and his people when they overran Israel. Malicious intentions were fostered by the prince. Many things came into his mind, and among them a special "evil thought." "It shall come to pass that at the same time shall things come into thy mind, and thou shalt think an evil thought." His intention was to go up against the defenceless, "to take a spoil and to take a prey." God rebuked him and threatened that "Divine fury should come in his face." Evil thoughts reveal

our characters and bring Divine condemnation.
God looks at the thoughts, and measures the
man by his thoughts.

The same thing is taught in the twenty-third
chapter of Proverbs. It commences with a direction as to how we are to act when invited to
dine with one above us in station. The guest is
to avoid over-indulgence. He is even to beware
of the pressure put upon him by the host to eat
and drink more freely. He is not to be led
away by the outward show of hospitality when
there may be hidden meanness. "Eat and
drink, saith he; but his heart is not with thee."
Then the sacred word lays down a canon whereby
we may judge of sterling character,—"For as
he thinketh in his heart, so is he." *The general
current of a man's thoughts determines his character.*

All men have a character of some sort. It is
something that attaches itself to us as closely
as our shadow. We cannot separate ourselves
from the one any more than from the other.
Even those who have by their acts lost all claim
to the esteem of their fellows have a character,
in that they are regarded as characterless.
Scouted by society on account of their vices,
they may wander hither and thither, but everywhere their known lack of character will follow
them. It is not the opinion of their fellows that
can stamp them, but their character depends
upon *what they are to themselves.* There are
those who may be accounted as only fit for

slander and shame, but who may yet be sterling; whereas, others who may be spoken of as
the purest and noblest, may be the meanest and
lowest. We would not be understood as affirm-
ing that a man is either wholly good or entirely
bad. The character of each is a compound. The
lines of slate and shale will often mingle in the
richest stratum of coal; and the vein of silver
may be found in the roughest mass of rock. The
general tone of the thoughts determines the real
character, whether of the Prince of Meshech or
a peasant of the mountains.

Now we must beware of thinking that a mere
outward pleasant manner, and genial temperament, are all that is requisite in a man of sterling character. Let us not make this mistake,
but seek to understand what are the *constituents*
of a really sterling character.

In a man of real worth there will be *transparency of life.* He will be easily seen through,—
not in the sense of being detected, but of being
so upright that there shall be nothing wrong to
detect. His every word will mean what it con-
veys, and his every action be performed from a
right motive, and not from such selfish thoughts
as those of the Prince of Meshech. Such an
one will be above the general suspiciousness
that is cherished by many. Neither will he
manifest great reserve. Ofttimes those who are
seeking to outwit and circumvent others, cultivate reservedness of manner the better to accomplish their purpose. Reserve often grows out of

selfishness. It begets reserve in others. Selfishness never dares to be transparent. It loves not the clear bright sunshine, but the damp and gloom. It flourishes best under the miasma of a suspicious, close and narrow spirit. The thoughts being mean, selfish, unprincipled, so will the man be. But the man of sterling character will so live, that if his thoughts were openly read by his fellows he would not be ashamed. *Pure-mindedness* alone can lead to transparency of life. It will be a transparency worth having,—for there are different degrees of transparency. Some only pretend to be transparent, like the cobwebbed, unwashed, dust-covered window, opening into some close alley. These affect an openness of life, and yield to practices of which it would be a shame to speak. Others are transparent, because pure; and are like the beautiful rose-window in the Cathedral at Amiens, where there is such a charming combination of colours that even the sun's rays passing through it are tinged with a brighter glory.

Again, in the man of sterling character there will be a *ready recognition of the supremacy of conscience*. There must be no loose notions on this point. Some would say that we must not be "over-particular," that we must be ready to "strain a point at times." It might sometimes be inconvenient to raise questions, and they "ask no questions," really "for conscience' sake." It might involve sacrifices for which they are not prepared. They will tell you that it does

4

not always *pay* to be too scrupulous. How could they then, like the Prince of Meshech, attack the defenceless or spoil the unprepared! Moreover, they will say that you must make allowance for circumstances, and that sometimes these will compel a man to act otherwise than he would strictly approve. Circumstances compel! Never, against conscience! Can any think thus "in their hearts?" then circumstances are their masters, they are slaves, and are ready to be driven to any length of sin if only circumstances are strong enough.

Too many have double consciences, one for church life, the other for commerce; one for the sanctuary, the other for the shop and the counting-house. They forget that that which they approve in the one must be carried out in the other. If they have principles, let them cling to them; if they claim to be men of sterling worth, let them bow ever before conscience.

See what honour the tempted Joseph, in Egyptian bondage, gained by clinging to principle. Said he, "How can I do this great wickedness, and sin against God?"

See how Moses, tempted to accept the pleasures of court life and a position of high state in Egypt,—tempted to hide his descent from the despised Israelites,—tempted to leave them in the brickfields of slavery under the rods of their taskmasters, "esteemed the reproach of Christ greater riches than the treasures of Egypt." He bowed to conscience and to God.

See how the Apostles, when before the high Jewish court, asserted the supremacy of conscience. They replied to the priests wishing to silence them, " Whether it be right in the sight of God to hearken unto you more than unto God, judge ye. We cannot but speak the things which we have seen and heard."

See how Luther asserted the same, before the mighty assembly convened by an emperor in the interest of the Papacy, at that critical moment " on which, as on a pivot, turned " the welfare of the Church. He said, " It is not right for a Christian to do anything against his conscience."

See, too, how John Hampden acted when our nation was in danger of being enslaved for generations to tyrants and to priestly power. To pay the ship tax, which had been unlawfully levied, would have been easy. It was but a trifle. Interest said "pay." Conscience, however, said " don't pay." He saw that the " worth of a principle is not determined by the extent of that which embodies it." "An apple to Newton and a kite to Franklin represented and suggested the great laws of Nature," so this trifle of ship money represented an attempt to undermine a great law of England, namely, that money should not be levied by the King without the consent of the Commons. Shall Hampden yield, or shall he take up a position of antagonism to his monarch, and be the means of unsettling the whole country by his refusal? Interest and some of his friends said " yield," but conscience made itself heard. He bowed to its supremacy. He would *not* pay.

And it was in obedience to this supremacy of conscience that those noble men, who sailed in the little *Mayflower*, went forth. Interest said, " Worship God as you are commanded by the King and government. Hear the book of sports, or anything else ; you need not approve or consent to all you hear." " No!" said these men. " God is a Spirit, and we will worship Him as our conscience directs. We will not, by our presence, consent to that of which in our hearts we disapprove." The spirit of these men, and of all those I have mentioned, must be in us if we would be men of real worth. Conscience must be ever supreme.

Further, in the man of sterling character there must ever be a *recognition of the value, and the actual possession of, real piety.* What are our thoughts in this respect? Some will possibly suggest that a man may be of sterling worth without religion. They may think of religion as only so much cant. They confound the one with the other. There have been men possessed of high moral qualities who gave no outward recognition of religion ; but if they were really moral they must have been under religious training or influence at some time or other. We know not where to look for specimens of those who are so good without religion. We fancy the species is rather rare. However

good men may appear who disown the influences
of religion, we may be very sure that they
would be none the worse for its possession.
Leave piety out of David's character, and
what would be left? Leave it out of those
of Peter or Paul, of James or John, and
we ask the same question. The "finishing
touch," the "top stone" of their character was
their piety. Morality apart from reverence for
God is self-glory. It may even produce pride.
Pride generally takes up its abode where piety
is not enshrined. Pride hides from us our real
state in God's sight. Pride hinders from the
acceptance of the Gospel of love and mercy. A
Christian may have pride in his nature, but he
struggles against it and seeks to gain the
mastery. However imperfect, he has this advantage, that he knows his failures and con-
fesses them. He seeks at the same time to
overcome them. But the man who claims to
be moral without being religious, who neglects
prayer, who can sneer at spiritual struggles,
who can treat the wondrous love of our Heavenly
Father with indifference, and the vicarious
sufferings of the tender-hearted Jesus with cold-
ness—however he may be applauded by his
fellows, is not the man of sterling character
we should desire to meet, for " As he thinketh
in his heart," on this subject, "so is he."
Further, the man of sterling character *must
love truth and purity for their own sake.* To
be good because it brings gain, or pious because

it pays, or religious because it is respectable, is hypocrisy.   There are inseparable advantages attaching to the possession of good character. Solomon said, "A good name is better than precious ointment."   Even a wretched trickster of the last century said, " I would give a thousand pounds any minute for a good character." He added in an undertone, " Because I could speedily make ten thousand of it."   Not for such sordid advantage, but for itself, should we value character.   Men ever respect those who respect themselves.   They will say of such, as of Joseph, when a man was needed to guide the affairs of Egypt during its frightful period of famine, "Can we find such an one as this is, a man in whom the spirit of God is *!*"   The Divine approval will be followed by men's approval, and in this the reward of character will come. But apart from this, we should seek to be true, noble, and pious, for the sake of goodness and truth itself.

We must not merely set up this as the standard at which we are to aim, and neglect to indicate the way in which true purity of character may be obtained.   Many may feel the desire stirring within to answer to all we have suggested, and yet they feel that they are imperfect, and they know not how to overcome evil.   The desired possession will not be obtained as by some "lucky stroke of business."   It must *grow.*   To obtain it among our fellows is easy when we deserve it. A steady course of uprightness and purity will bring it. We must not be spasmodic in our goodness. We must *watch little things,* avoid habits that offend in the slightest degree. Getting rid of these things, we must *retain our individuality.* We must not measure ourselves by other persons and think because we live just after the same manner, and on the same moral plane as some others, that therefore we are good enough. There are higher possibilities in the nature of each. There is room for, and should be *enthusiasm*—enthusiasm for the truth, for the welfare of humanity, for the glory of God our Father, and of Christ our Saviour. Do not be afraid of being enthusiastic. Let the fire burn in your soul. Mean to be and to do something. Get stimulus from any source that is right. *Read good books.* A single book may change or colour your whole life. It was concerning a certain book that an Italian gentleman wrote, "If I had read that book earlier in life, my whole life would have been altogether a different thing."

But in thus speaking of other books I would throw no slight on the grandest book of any, the Bible. We must read, and should read, other books at times, but in *The* Book we have recorded the noblest biography of all, the highest example set up, that of Jesus. It is said of Him that He "*grew* in wisdom and stature, and in favour with God and men." He was the type of what life should be, pure, self-denying, and obedient to our Father's will in all things. Who can ever gaze upon the perfect, harmonious and loving life of Jesus without feeling humbled beyond measure at the contrast presented by his own frail, disjointed, sinful and imperfect life? Nothing, my friends, teaches us more forcibly the need for a renewal of nature, a change of heart, than seeing the contrast presented by what Christ was and what we are. When we have come to Him and have found the pardon and peace which may be ours through His great sacrificial work, we can be strong in principle and sterling in character. As we keep near to Him, and have His example ever before us, we shall grow. Let but the Spirit of Christ dwell in us, and then, as

> "Some rare perfume in vase of clay,
> Pervades it with a fragrance not its own,"

so our lives and characters shall partake of a sweetness and beauty approved by men and acceptable to God.

The Prince of Meshech had those around him who were ready to approve his dastardly intention, when he said, "I will go up to the land of unwalled villages; I will go to them that are at rest, that dwell safely, all of them dwelling without walls, and having neither gates nor bars, to take a spoil and to take a prey." The mind is coloured by the thoughts and sayings of those surrounding us, even as the lake is blue or greyish according to the qualities of the mountains down the sides of which the streams and torrents flow that fill it. How important

then that we should *seek to associate chiefly
with Christians,* and ever keep ourselves surrounded by Christian influences. There is a
Persian fable which tells us that a man one day
picked up a piece of scented clay, and said to it,
—" What are you ; are you musk ? " " No, I
am only a poor piece of clay, but I have been
near a beautiful rose, and it has given me its
own sweet smell." Keep, therefore, in the
society of the good, and live as near as possible
to Christ, and then you will gain such purity
and nobility of nature that the world will take
knowledge of you that you have been with Him.
A character will be yours, such as may even
make up for lack of genius or great talents.
You, by mere consistency of character, may then
do in the shop and society as much good as one
who has unbounded wealth, wide influence, great
power of speech, activity of thought, and opportunities of utterance in the church and world.

Let me say that we should *beware of seeking
to build up character in our own strength.* If
we attempt it we shall find that we have
chosen a sandy foundation. A few of the
storms of life it may withstand, but when the
shock of the judgment day shall come, and the
dread of an unknown future shall break upon
us, we shall surely be swept away. Christ's
example, Christ's sacrifice, Christ's pardon,
Christ's help, Christ's love, Christ Himself, in
the fulness of His power, these form the only true
and safe foundation.

It is the character of Him whom we serve that should stir us to purity, nobility, and manliness. That which nerves a soldier's arm, and strengthens a soldier's heart, is not the number of the army, but the character of the general he follows and obeys. Those who followed the Prince of Meshech would soon be disorganized and demoralized. A mean leader cannot inspire respect, but a true and noble man fills others with courage. It is said that in one of the Duke of Wellington's battles, a portion of the army, under a heavy charge of cavalry, wavered and was giving way. Most opportunely, at that moment, the Duke rode into the very midst of the wavering ranks. One of the soldiers who had often fought under the Duke descried him, and shouted in joyous tones, "There's the Duke, God bless him! I had rather see his face than see a whole brigade." All eyes turned quickly to the chief. They knew they were looking on one who knew not how to yield, and who had oft turned apparent defeat into victory. Under this assurance they repulsed their foes and "turned the battle to the gate." Thus the knowledge that we belong to Christ, and are His followers, should so inspire us that a glance at Him will always nerve our arms, and enable us to overcome every difficulty in the way of attaining the purity of character I have portrayed.

We have a good test as to what is our real character in this—in our loving Christ and the things

of Christ. Several old tables of brass are still
standing opposite the Exchange, in one of the
principal streets of Bristol; and these tables must
have caused many to ask, "What purpose do they
serve?" Unable, some time ago, to make out their
use, I enquired of a friend. He told me—and
possibly the explanation may be the right one
—that in former times, when the merchants
received payment for their goods, it was their
custom to take the money outside, and, by
dashing each piece on these brazen testers,
discover whether the money was genuine or
counterfeit. Thus I have pointed out the
means whereby we may test our characters.
Let us avoid having the hardness of a Meshech
or the meanness of the urgent host.

Let us not hide it from ourselves if we know
we are not true, sincere, open and sterling
in character. Hiding the fact does not alter it,
any more than when the ostrich hides its head
in the sand it becomes proof against the shots
of the hunter. We have no wish to make out
any to be worse than they are, but we do
wish to stimulate them to seek to become nobler
and purer. Let all strive *"to be what they wish
to appear."* Let us strive even to see ourselves
in heaven's pure light. It may be annoying to
find that here and there are failures and weaknesses which we had not suspected; humbling
to find that sins are not conquered when we
had thought we were rid of them; dishearten-
ing to find we have still to maintain a severe

conflict; but away with all self-deception.   Let
us seek to know and see ourselves as we shall do
when we pass from this world into the blaze of
light in that world where self-deception will be
impossible.   Let us *pray* that God will help us
to be all we should be, and if possible *better
than others suspect.*   To pray and to wish is to
will.   *To will is to be.*   To desire and to will
to be transparent, conscientious, pious, prayer-
ful, manly, and truly christian, is to be of
sterling worth.   It must be a sincere desire
and an earnest willing, or all is useless.

God help us all to be true and to throw
away everything that is worthless.   God help us
to avoid thinking "an evil thought" like that
of the Prince of Meshech.   God help us to
"keep our hearts with all diligence," because
"out of them are the issues of life."

HUSHAI, THE ARCHITE; OR A FATEFUL MEETING.

SCRIPTURE REFERENCE—II. *Sam.* xv. 32.

WHAT changes and vicissitudes come in life! See what David had been: shepherd, warrior, poet, harpist, courtier, and king. He had been loved, honoured, feared, and now he is driven from home and throne, flees before his son as an enemy, and has to bear with the bitter curses and the stone-throwing of a Shimei. He is forsaken by many, but adhered to by a brave and faithful few, such as Jonathan, Ahimaaz, and Hushai the Archite, or Archevite, a native of Erech. [cf. Gen. x, 10; Joshua xvi, 2; Ezra iv, 9.]

Hushai strongly wished to accompany David, to whom he was deeply attached. He was troubled greatly at the calamity which had overtaken the king, and the latter was equally troubled to think of the pain and inconvenience Hushai must suffer for his sake in following his changed fortunes. David knew also that Hushai

could do better service for him by remaining in
the city and counteracting by judicious counsel
some of the evil intentions of Absalom. He
has great difficulty in persuading Hushai to
remain, and has to appear almost rude and
even ungrateful in the effort to accomplish his
desire. He could bear anything for himself,
but he could not permit another to undergo
such exhausting experiences for his sake.
Hence he puts as his final argument this
strong sentence, "If thou passest over with
me thou wilt be a burden."

David suggested that Hushai should assume
the character of a friend of Absalom. The suggestion must not be measured by present
standards of morality. At that time it would
be thought quite lawful to endeavour to
circumvent an opponent by placing a spy in
his court, even as at this day some triumph of
diplomacy would be extolled by politicians.

David had a lingering hope that in some
way Hushai might be able to save his son. He
felt sure he would be able to defeat the counsel
of Ahithophel, the one most likely to lead
Absalom further astray. Hence he urged and
insisted on Hushai's return.

Almost at the *same moment* the Archite and
Absalom enter the city; the one in silence, the
other with pomp; the one aged and depressed,
the other young and elate; one sorrowing over
the treatment of David, the other rejoicing over
his easy success. Soon the two are face to face.

Absalom meets his fate. The meeting was as significant as some that have taken place later in history, as that for instance between Philip and William, afterwards named the Silent. To him Philip confided casually the knowledge of his intention to exterminate all the Protestants of the two countries, and William, while startled and saddened at the information gave no sign, but mentally determined to counteract the intended cruelty. Philip met his fate in William the Silent, and Absalom met his when he came in contact with Hushai.

There is in the account of this meeting an illustration of how *sometimes we may find unexpectedly useful guidance.* Hushai might have been a useful guide, but Absalom is bent on evil, and Ahithophel helps him in his wickedness. Hushai only seeks to defeat the evil counsel of the latter. This he attempts for David's sake, as well as Absalom's. Absalom could, if he had been true, have had a most valuable counsellor in Hushai, but under the circumstances, all Hushai can do is to endeavour to help David, or to give him time to escape, by counselling delay on the part of Absalom.

Life is like a many-tracked common or heath; so many paths run side by side or cross each other at different angles. We pass numberless wanderers like ourselves, but here and there we meet casually with some one who is most useful, because he chances to know the direction of the paths, and a word at a perplexing juncture is invaluable. For such guidance we are thankful. Absalom had in Hushai one who would have done his best to counsel him for good, but his heart was set on evil, so that Hushai's influence was unavailing.

A *warning* also came to the rebellious son in that meeting. If David yesterday was followed, loved, and trusted, and is to-day forsaken and hunted, so might he be served when the flush of success has faded. Those now so warm in his interest might leave him even as Hushai had turned back from David. Had not he been known preeminently as "David's friend," and now he is giving countenance to the king's enemy. Absalom needed the warning just then, for he was contemplating most dastardly crimes. Just as Hushai meets him unexpectedly, so retribution may meet him also, at the point where he seems to have reached the full extent of his expectations of success. There is indeed that which a French writer calls *force cachée*, or hidden power, checking us often at the very moment of success wrongly gained. It is not always noticed, but sometimes it comes, startling us with its suddenness. Ahab goes down to seize the vineyard of Naboth, and at the door Elijah meets him with the sentence, "In the place where dogs licked the blood of Naboth, shall dogs lick thy blood, even thine." The courtiers who wrought against Daniel were

themselves doomed to the death they designed for him. A cardinal introduced iron
cages into France, and was afterwards himself
imprisoned in one. A man who during the
first revolution in France, was condemned to
death by the criminal tribunal of Lyons, was
the first to suffer under the very guillotine
that he had sent for from Paris to decapitate
his enemies. The poisoned chalice prepared for
another is in tragedy represented as being
unwittingly drunk by the Danish King and
Queen. The bell put up by the good Abbot
of Aberbrothok on Inchcape Rock is represented
by the great Scottish novelist as having been
taken down by a pirate, and he, a year after,
being unwarned, perished on that very rock.

" Stories have been told of men whose lives
  Were infamous, and so their end.   I mean
  That the red-handed murderer has himself been murdered:
  The traitor struck with treason :   he who let
  The orphan perish came himself to want.
  Thus justice and the great God have ordered it
  So that the scene of evil has been turned
  Against the actor ;   pain paid back with pain,
  And poison given for poison."

If in secular history we discover the opera-
tion of this *force cachée*, how much more in
sacred.   There the working of the law is laid
down thus :   "The wicked shall fall by his
own naughtiness ;" the ungodly falls into the
net he spreads for his neighbour's feet.

Absalom in meeting with Hushai comes in contact with one who will lead him into the pit he had dug for his father and king. There was a divine hand in this, and in the after consultation, when the advice of Ahithophel failed, and that of Hushai was taken. God worked through words. The Lord "had appointed" to defeat that counsel. The whole circumstances recorded in the sixteenth chapter are deeply interesting. That for which Hushai strove was to gain time for David to get over Jordan. To have a few hours, advantage in a march, or for arranging forces, may decide the fate of a war. David has right on his side. He has God on his side. Soon he will also have victory on his side. " For whom," said Luther, " Do ye hold God ; for a cypher ?" Many forget that God is an active and righteous God, and that when trying to carry out their evil designs they may meet with an unexpected check, even as Absalom did when coming in contact with Hushai.

To dare to indulge in sin is as unwise as to go and lie down on the rails along which a train is rapidly approaching. Consequences which we think far off come up silently and swiftly, dazing and paralysing us by their terrible aspect. Perhaps the result of some sin committed years ago is even now quietly and surely approaching us. Only God can save us from our sins and deliver us from their consequences. Absalom sought not deliverance, but rushed blindly on, not knowing that he had met his fate in Hushai.

This momentous meeting between the rebellious son and the father's friend may lead us to think of other coincident meetings that have had a very different result. We might think of the meeting of the woman of Samaria with Christ at Sychar's well; or of that of Zaccheus, who pushing aside the thick leaves of the tree he had ascended the better to see Jesus, found that He, whom he had gone out curiously to see, wished to abide that day at his house; or of the thief who met Christ on the strange hill of Golgotha, and found that the words of his wondrous companion in suffering eased his pain, and made the cross a gate to heaven; or of Saul going to Damascus, boiling with bitterness and blatant with threats, meeting with Him, the radiance of whose face eclipsed the light of heaven, and the force of whose enquiry, "Saul, Saul, why persecutest thou Me?" changed the whole current of his life, making of the savage zealot a humble Christian, and of the emissary of the Sanhedrim the untiring missionary of the cross, the "chosen vessel to suffer great things" for his Master. That same Christ is ever waiting to meet with any soul that desires His love, and is willing to trust for eternal salvation in the sacrifice offered by Him on Calvary. Still He waits! Who will meet Him?

THE YOUNG LEVITE; OR, RICH CONTENT.

SCRIPTURE REFERENCES—*Judges* xvii, 2; *Acts* ii, 46.

IN the days when "there was no king in Israel," and when every man did that which was right in his own eyes, a man of Mount Ephraim, named Micah, stole from his mother eleven hundred shekels of silver. After confessing his crime, his mother told him that she had dedicated the silver to the Lord, to make therewith "a graven image and a molten image." Micah the thief now became the god-maker. He had soon "a house of gods," an "ephod," and "teraphim." He knew that he was not fitted to act himself as priest, and therefore set apart one of his sons for the office. This son filled the office until a young Levite, who had wandered away from home seeking for some suitable abiding-place, chanced to come that way when Micah engaged him as priest. The god-owner, the man who had entered into a sort of religious speculation, saw that if he had one who, though not a priest, was yet officially connected with the tabernacle services, as his chaplain or arch-priest, it would be to the advantage of his speculation. He knew that his shrine would become more popular, and his profits from free gifts greater. He agreed to give the young Levite a certain sum, "his apparel and his victuals." Then it is said that "the Levite was content to dwell with the man, and he became to Micah as one of his sons." The young Levite remained contentedly with Micah until a band of Danites stole Micah's silver gods and invited him to come with them, and be priest to the tribe. Then we are told that "the priest's heart was glad, and he took the ephod, and the teraphim, and the graven image, and went in the midst of the people." His morals were bad, but his spirit of general contentedness was good. He was content with Micah, and just as content afterwards with the Danites.

Can it be said of men now that they are content? How much unrest is there all around us! With what eager, anxious countenances do men move about the world! How hurried is life! With what intensity do men pursue wealth, power, and fame. The man of the world acts on the principle contained in the words of Horace, "Give me health and wealth, and I will not ask Jove himself to give me content." It is supposed that the latter is sure to come with the possession of the former. Vain expectation! A man's poverty or wealth is not

determined by what he has, but by the fulness
of his content. Thus, a poor man may be really
rich, and a rich man poor indeed.

The discontented spirit is easily discovered.
The merchant, in his office or on the market,
makes certain profits, but frets himself that he
has not made more. The tradesman bitterly complains of the badness of trade, and the artizan
of slackness of work. When he has succeeded
in finding employment he will be found quarrell-
ing with the rate of payment. Nor is the
discontented spirit confined to the town; it is
found in rural districts too. We admire the
homestead nestling under the shelter of the
hills; we notice the trellised porch, the ivy-
clad walls, the trim garden, and the smoothly-
cut lawn. Appearances tell only of beauty,
peace, and comfort; yet here, perhaps, we may
find domestic misery, or grumbling, or passion,
rife. Speak with the occupier, and what a string
of complaints he has about home or weather;
speak with the wife, and she complains of her
wayward family; with the son, and you find
that he is weary of country life, and longs for
the excitement of a city; with the daughter,
and she is annoyed that school life has to be
followed by what she terms "home drudgery."
You may go away from such a place of beauty
in complete disgust. The appearances have
completely belied the reality. Even among
those who have, seemingly, few wants, it is
almost as bad. Even the Indian, for whom a

blanket and weapon would appear to suffice, is ofttimes discontented because game is scarce or his maize plot unproductive. It is difficult to find any person who is without some reason for discontent, or any position which places a man beyond its reach. From the mendicant to the monarch, all have some unsatisfied longing, some cause of envy or jealousy which hinders them from living with contentedness of mind.

In the latter part of the second chapter of the Acts of the Apostles, we are told that the early converts did " eat their meat with single-ness of heart." Whether at home, partaking of the ordinary meal, or joining, at the solemn gathering, in the sacred observance of the Lord's Supper, one thing was remarked in their conduct, that all was done with "singleness of heart," *i.e.* with simplicity of spirit.

The joy of the early Church grew out of its contentedness. Its first experience of the results of religion was so joyous that it was a foretaste of millennial bliss. It lasted, unfortunately, too short a time, and yet long enough to show what should be the ideal of life.

The phrase, " singleness of heart," is used in connection with eating. Possibly there is no-thing in which the lack of this simplicity of heart might be noticed more plainly than in the way in which men dispatch their ordinary meals. Some eat like the Israelites, "in haste," with their " loins girded." Life seems at such fever heat with them that they have not time to supply it with the fuel for combustion. They are so eager to become rich, to advance in knowledge, to gain position or fame, and to surpass others, that they eat not in "singleness of heart." They rather keep the heart in a constant turmoil of desires, and the brain in an unceasing fret. No wonder that the physical frame breaks down, and that sometimes the mental organization becomes deranged.

This "simplicity of heart," this contentedness of mind, is not always inherited, does not always come by nature, but *may be obtained*. It can only come fully when the heart is at peace with God through Christ. When, through the atoning work of Christ, a man sees not only his sinfulness and need of pardon, but what a claim God has upon all his services, and when he resolves to respond to the claim, he will find peace, and live in contentedness of spirit. The will is brought into harmony with the Divine will. The soul, emptied of its pride and self-righteousness, rests only in the mercy of God and the grace of the Holy Spirit. The man is "alive to God." He gives all his affection to God, because he lives in the love which God has to him. He finds in himself still many tendencies to sin, but he seeks to trample them under foot in Christ's strength. His greatest desire is to have his whole nature subdued to Christ, and serve Him in "singleness of heart."

Again, this state is not one which comes to all suddenly. Indeed, it comes to most *gradually*.

Paul, the apostle, only attained it by degrees. He said, " I have *learned* in whatsoever state I am, therewith to be content." He was converted suddenly, on the outskirts of Damascus, but he found afterwards that he had something still to learn, " to follow after," to " seek," " to apprehend," and to " attain." If a Paul had to learn to be content, and study to acquire "singleness of heart," shall we expect to attain thereunto by some spasmodic and brief effort !

There is a temporary *advantage in discontent.* But for dissatisfaction with our spiritual state and progress, we should not strive to make any advance. Indeed, nearly all advance is the result of discontent. If men had habitually rested content with things as they were, we should not have had the material advantages we now possess. We had had fewer comforts ; less facility for the transport of food, or for personal travel by steamship and rail ; no mills to weave our garments, or electric wires to flash our messages. These have all been successive outcomes of discontent with the existing state of things. Grumbling will not bring to the cultivator suitable weather ; but in spiritual matters to grumble may be to grow. Therefore, discontent with our spiritual state is one means of advancing to that state in which the commonest acts of life are done to God's glory.

Look at some of the results which follow the attainment of the contented spirit. There will be *a readiness to make the best of any position in which we may be placed.* Men often fancy that if they were in some other position than that which they occupy, they would be better in character, much happier, and able to do much more for God. The best guarantee of the probability of any such improvement is to be found in the way in which we use our present position. It is well to cultivate contentedness in respect to our position in life, if it be one where we can have health, spiritual advantages, and opportunities of doing that which shall glorify God. Note the reply of Barzillai, the Gileadite,—who had befriended David when fleeing from a rebellious son,—when invited afterwards to go up to Jerusalem to dwell with the king: "How long have I to live, that I should go up with the king unto Jerusalem? . . Let thy servant, I pray thee, turn back again, that I may die in mine own city, and be buried by the grave of my father and of my mother." Remember, too, what the Shunammite woman said to Elisha, when he asked her whether, in return for all her kindness, she would be "spoken for to the king or to the captain of the host?" Her reply was brief, but suggestive of divine content: "I dwell among mine own people." Sometimes you may meet with individuals who now possess a similar contentedness of spirit and "singleness of heart." There was a schoolmaster among the Cumberland Hills, of whom Robertson speaks in one of his lectures—a man who rested content with a very small school, small salary, and small house ; though his abilities would have obtained for him a position much higher in the eyes of the world, but who refused every inducement to remove. He said, "I reckon that the privilege of living amid beautiful scenery much more than compensates for a large salary, with work in the stifling atmosphere of some town." It is possible, therefore, to gain contentedness in respect to position, and the more surely if we can have the assurance that Christ has taken up His abode in our hearts.

Where this spirit obtains, there will be a *more cheerful view of life cherished.* Gloom makes the wheels of life to drag ; cheerfulness silences creaking, and makes things move smoothly. The road of life is generally rough enough, so that we need not make it more difficult to traverse by our complaining and croaking. God would not have us gloomy and wretched. He is happy in His love to men and efforts for them, and He would have us happy in His mercy and salvation. When our sins are forgiven, and souls accepted in Christ, we may be cheerful. We may rejoice, nay, we are commanded "to rejoice :" —to rejoice "evermore."

A little child once enquired, "Mamma, did the cheerful God make all the beautiful flowers ?" The child's idea of God was one far higher than that of many Christians. Her expression, which was apparently bold, was one indicative of sweet simplicity and "singleness

of heart." Would that we could be in spirit
as that little child.

Where this spirit of content obtains, there
will be a *more earnest performance of any duty
that may fall upon us.* That which our hands
find to do we shall do with our might. We shall
ever search out occasions of usefulness. If we see
any wrong, we shall not be content to let it rest.
If we see ignorance and sin around, we shall
strive to remove it. We shall ask ourselves
whether the condition of our fellows in the rural
districts and in the crowded parts of our great
towns and cities is such as God would have?
We shall ask ourselves whether we can do anything to put away from their minds the notion
that the well-to-do care not for them? We shall
strive to make allowance for ignorance, wasteful-
ness, evil habits, and even for duplicity. We
shall seek to elevate and bless them. We shall
" hope all things," and become more sympathetic
both to those at home, around us, and far away.
We shall want to do something for them, because
we shall see in them souls for whom Christ died,
for whose sanctification the Holy Spirit was
given, and over whom, when redeemed, the
angels would rejoice. We should not be able
to think of all the misery and sin of the world
without striving to do something to alleviate it.
Some seldom think—

> " Of the hearts that daily break,
>   Of the tears that hourly fall,
>   Of the many, many troubles of life,
>   That grieve this earthly ball."

Content with their own lot, they have not sought to help others. Too late they have to come to the regretful conclusion of the one whom the poet represents as saying—

> " Alas, I have walked through life,
> Too heedless where I trod;
> Nay, helping to trample my fellow-worms,
> And fill the burial sod;
> Forgetting that even the sparrows' fall
> Is not unmarked by God.

> " The wounds I might have healed!
> The human sorrow and smart!
> And yet it never was in my soul
> To play so ill a part:
> But evil is wrought by want of thought,
> As well as by want of heart."

Where there is this rich content and true "singleness of heart" *there will be a clearer and yet clearer perception of God's truth and will.* When the mind is filled with prejudices, the judgment will be warped, and the truth hidden. " He that will do His will shall know of the doctrine." There is a clearness of vision following on " singleness " of desire. There is also a jaundice of the mind as well as of the body. Of this we shall beware. We shall simply come to God's Word and seek to know what is right. Being spiritually minded, we shall " compare " and " discern " the spiritual. We shall not desire to take God's Word in any unnatural sense, on the one hand; nor accept a narrow interpretation, on the other. The heart will be a better guide than the head in understanding God's will and Word.

Moreover, there will be *perfect willingness to leave everything in God's hands.* Much of the fret and worry of life will thus be saved. We shall believe that He, in whom we live and move and have our being, He, who redeemed us at such a cost as the gift of His own well-beloved Son, will so over-rule our lives that they shall not be cast away as worthless ; that He will "choose our inheritance" for us, and " determine the bounds of our habitation." We shall thus keep the " restless will " under, and shall be content to follow the path our Heavenly Father marks out. When we cannot see the marking ; when we are like travellers through Canadian dense forests, who can see no sun through the thick foliage, and who can detect no trail or even the markings, called a " blaze", on the trees, we shall still trust. When we are like such travellers, going round and round among trees seeking some outlet, but making no progress, we shall still have faith in God. When our path is blocked by circumstances, as a sleigh by the heavy snow-fall ; or when we are encompassed by fog or darkness, we shall still rest in God. Knowing that our heart is firmly "fixed," we shall be ready to say—

> " Keep Thou my feet, I do not ask to see
> The distant scene ; one step's enough for me."

Let us cultivate all patience, hopefulness, and charity. Out of all evils some good may be drawn. The true Christian believes this, and therefore, when trials and perplexities come he leaves all to God. He is thus enabled to dwell

in the " Land of Thankfulness " instead of the
" Country of Complaint." The latter is a land
of fog and gloom, but the former is a sweet, well-
watered region, where gleam the green pastures
that David loved, and where flow the rivers of
content, by which Paul dwelt; where the valleys abound in springs of hope, and the hills are
clad with the fruits of spiritual joy, where the
sunshine of Divine love brightens all circumstances of trial or difficulty, and gives constant
assurance of future glory.

It is possible to dwell in this land of joy and
thankfulness even now. Not only have psalm-
ists and apostles dwelt there, but many humble
and sincere believers whose names will never be
known to the world. An account is given by
Dr. Watts of the experience of John Howe, the
eminent puritan divine, and chaplain to Cromwell. Once when he had been preaching to his
people, and largely insisting on the passage,
" For our rejoicing is this, the testimony of our
conscience," &c. (2 Cor. i. 12), afterwards a " wonderful and copious stream of celestial rays, from
the lofty throne of divine majesty, did seem to
dart into his expanded breast." Howe says that
he experienced " an inexpressible pleasant melt-
ing of heart; tears gushed out of his eyes for
joy that God should shed abroad His love
through the hearts of men, and that for this
very purpose his own heart should be so sig-
nally possessed of and by His blessed Spirit."
This may seem extravagant to some who

have never known such intense joy; but if ever there was a man who lived in "singleness of heart," in rich contentedness of spirit, and who sought in all things God's glory, that man was John Howe, of Torrington, and it is not extravagance for him thus to speak. This is only one instance of how God gives great joy to those who seek and serve Him in singleness of heart. Let all ask themselves whether they have had such joy? If they have not, let them seek it. Let them also be assured that such joy can only come where the Saviour is absolutely trusted for pardon, and God is served simply from love.

THE SON OF NER;

OR DISAPPOINTED EXPECTATIONS.

SCRIPTURE REFERENCE.—II *Sam*. iii. 39.

VERY stormy period of David's life was just closing; he had been hunted as a "partridge upon the mountains." Endless had been the plottings of Saul. David had been in danger from javelins at feasts and emissaries in the home. He, however, kept his hand from being lifted up against Saul. Exiled, he waited in the land of Philistia until the proper time should come for his return. He waited for a crown. His was truly a "divine right," because given by direct prophetical appointment, and because he had proved it by the prowess and patience manifested. It was hard to have been driven about so many years, his very name spoken of with opprobrium. Saul, Nabal, and others spoke of him contemptuously as "the Son of Jesse." He had not sought the crown. There had been no plottings and schemings and "fusions" on his part. Even Jonathan recognised his right, and saw that, because of his father's sins, the crown was to pass from his house, probably never to revert to it again. As the heir apparent he had resigned his claim, and only asked that kindness should be shewn to his descendants. When, however, Jonathan and Saul were both dead, and there was nothing apparently to hinder David's assuming the throne, Abner, a powerful general, espoused the cause of Ishbosheth, the representative of the legitimate successor to the kingdom. Abner proclaimed him king at one end of the kingdom, while David was proclaimed at the other. David highly esteemed Abner, and could have wished that he had been in alliance with him. Unfortunately, as we surmise, there was some jealousy between Abner and another powerful general, Joab, and this jealousy was increased to hatred by another circumstance, the death of Joab's brother by the hand of Abner. Abner slew him unwillingly. He warned Asahel to turn aside from pursuing him. Joab, doubtless, often sought opportunity to be revenged on Abner, but none came, although " there was long time war between the house of Saul and the house of David."

Ishbosheth wrongly accused Abner; for he became somewhat lifted up because Abner had lately been stronger. Abner, annoyed, threatened a change. Great is the power of a military dictator. Without an army at his back, what can Ishbosheth do? He who claims to be a king is patronised, not the patron. Abner carried out his threat. Messengers were sent to David. Offers to turn Israel to the king were made. There was considerable flitting to and fro of political agents. Abner had to win over the different tribes to his project, and this was not easy. At length he succeeds, and the one hitherto an opponent meets David. Negotiations are complete. All Israel is to be gathered to make a league with David. Peace is established at last, and Abner leaves the city. He has not gone, however, far, when Joab comes back from pursuing a troop. He is laden with spoil and full of joy. Learning just then, to his annoyance, that Abner has been to Hebron and has been received with favour by the king, he determines to remove him. What, is he to have a rival in the king's favour? Is his rival to be the slayer of his brother? Is he no longer to be able to dictate to the king? Has he touched the zenith of his power, and must he now decline? He goes to the king. "What hast thou done?" Short question. Imperative manner. Then he puts a mean interpretation on Abner's motive, saying that he only came " to know all that thou doest."

There are various hints of how Joab presumed upon his position, and it is probable that David would have rejoiced to have had some one to counteract his influence, for it is never pleasant to be at the mercy of one man. Even a king was conscious of that. He promised himself extra strength in the adhesion of Abner. Joab, however, checkmated the King. He sent a message to Abner, and Abner returned to Hebron again. Joab meets him at the gate, and pretends to have something to say quietly to him ere he goes to the king. Then he smites him under the "fifth rib," so that he dies.

David disowns any share in the crime, and follows the bier as chief mourner; moreover, he pronounces at the grave an elegy in honour of Abner, then returns to weep and fast. To his attendants he afterwards speaks of the fallen general in terms of great praise. It is certainly not always what a man may say in public of another that is to be taken as a guide. Especially is this the case with the dead. Men who have despised others when living have sometimes,—if asked,—uttered the most laudatory oration over them when dead. Not so with David. He in public and private was the same. He had always honoured the son of Ner, though he had been compelled to fight against him. Mutual respect had been the offspring of mutual resistance. Hence, when Abner was to have been a friend, David promised himself much joy. Not only would a great difficulty be removed, but the king would have another brave man to help to strengthen his throne and keep back all his enemies. In *proportion* to a man's power to hinder so is his power sometimes to help. Abner would have been a strength. Losing him, David says, "I am weak this day, though anointed king."

Possibly the king by these words meant that a wrong opinion might be formed of him; that some might impute to him treachery. He knew the power of public opinion, and how scandal travels with electric swiftness. Hence, to have even a doubt thrown on his character made him say, " I am weak this day, though anointed king." David had certainly *attained* his desire. He now ruled over a united kingdom. The angel of peace was to spread her gentle wings over the land. The sword was no longer to devour. Alas, with the peace comes a death. Over his hopes a pall is spread. Into the cup of his rejoicings bitterness is dashed. A staggering sense of weakness comes over him while yet he is flushed with the glory of increased power. The loss of the Son of Ner was a calamity to the king.

Is it not the experience of men that *disappointments frequently follow upon the attainment of our hopes, and are often intermingled with them?* We know how men struggle for riches, and yet, when gained, they have often lost the power of enjoying them. For fame they struggle, and gain it possibly too late even to know of their success. The tree a man has planted in his youth, and for the fruit of which he has long waited, is ripening, and just then he loses the power to take or to taste it. Or, to change the figure, we might say, the argosy of good is coming into port, when the ship strikes the bar or is driven on the rocks, just at the entrance of the harbour. The crew and cargo may be saved, but the noble vessel, whose prow was power and whose form was beauty, will never again cleave the waters, or bear homewards the riches of distant shores. The topmost step of the throne is reached by David, the sceptre grasped, the crown is placed, but the pæan of joy is changed into the doleful note of sorrow.

This is not the *invariable* but *general* experience. It is so frequent that it might almost be accounted as a rule, having some exceptions, that disappointment shall intermingle with all attainment. Now this intermingled disappointment is a divine appointment. God intended it. He has so arranged it because there are advantages arising from such disappointments.

We have constant illustrations of this. Those who are *detained by sickness in their rooms* often widely influence others for good. Those who have to meet severe temptations find that strength is gained by resistance. The spiritual muscles become strong by use. Those who have to wield the hammer in moulding or making a sword, or to use the sword in beating back some evil, become strong by such efforts. Hence God has not promised that ease shall follow any course, that peace shall come directly a war has ceased.

How little moral power comes through a mere velvety life! The soft, low tones of cultivated effeminacy are not the tones that would be heard along the line of battle, stirring the soldiers' hearts when the clash of arms is fiercest

and when cannons roar their loudest. Some
may rise to heights of moral grandeur under the
southern clime of comfort and amid the breathings of the mild summer breeze; but if real
power is to be gained there must be trial,
difficulty, disappointment from within or from
without, and the head will often have to be
bent to the fierce and icy northern blast.

All have in joy some intermingling of sorrow.
One man has wealth, or position, or remarkable
powers, but who can tell of his longings,
jealousies, annoyances? He has great losses,
unrealized ideals, expectations, absence of sympathy, unreasonable tempers to withstand, and
perhaps unsuitable companionship. Though that
lady sits in silk and lolls in luxury she may know
the bitterness of unreturned affection; may find
that she has wasted life's dearest treasure on a
heart as worthless as withered leaves and dry as
summer's dust. To a woman whose whole life is
bound up in the possession of a husband's love,
what can be a more fearful trial than its loss,
even though should remain to her the accompaniments of a splendidly decked equipage and
richly appointed household? She might say,
"I am weak this day, though I sit as a
queen."

What a lesson for the successful or the
struggling. *Poverty, and weakness, and sickness, and solitude, have their counter-balanc-
ings.* Power may grow out of privation and
strength out of suffering, but ennui is the out-

come of pleasurable ease, and satiety of constant satisfaction. The strong must know moments of weakness. God has appointed this, for God would not have the weak crushed or the strong proud. All are to be *humble*, trustful ; to learn that all things are from Him.

One advantage arising from disappointment is that *we learn to make God our all.* All happiness has its alloy, and all sorrow its surcease. Joy in God alone is untouched. We must learn to say, "In the cross and Christ I glory." To have all joy in Him will perhaps cost us some pain. Self dies hard, very hard. The right eye may have to be plucked out, the right hand to be cut off, but anything that offends must go. How many things do offend ! How many things we have to regret ! Habits, desires, and sins are not put aside without struggle. The past is not easily forgotten. But the struggles and disappointments are beneficial. Spiritual *being and life* are thereby developed. We are driven more and more to rest in God. Then "all things are ours." What reck we of trials if God is ours and we are His ? We grow up into a sense of kingship. We are satisfied to be His children. We realize more and more that we are made priests and kings unto God.

This may lead us to notice that if in this life there is often the counter-balancing sorrow to the joy, it may be the same hereafter. Christ's words, "Thou in thy lifetime receivedst thy good things, etc.," teach a very solemn truth concerning the revelations of the future. Many will then get a clearer vision of what was the high meaning of the gospel, and will be ashamed that the record of their life was so meagre and the results so mean. If saved, they will wish they had done more for Christ and loved more their fellows. The very greatness of the glory, the very richness of the reward will make us feel the more keenly how unpardonable was our neglect, in that we were so little concerned for the progress of spiritual power and for the manifestation of Christ's love in the world.

These thoughts need not make us gloomy. If we can learn what is God's will we should be indeed cheerful. Little can we do if despondency seize us. If we should be weak, at least let us not bend our heads like bulrushes. God overrules the past. The cross of Christ alone is strength. Brighten then the world by reflecting Christ's image. Cheer it by telling of Christ's love.

Many are weak without realizing their weakness. David might have said, "Now I rejoice that I am strong, for an enemy has been removed from my path." Not so. Out of an enemy he would have fashioned a powerful friend. He knew what he had lost. Many know not what they lose in losing Christ and a Father's love. They have no stay in life, and no home hereafter. Homesickness must come ere we are impelled to start homewards. T he

prodigal must feel his weakness and desolation
while he remembers his sonship. Oh, that
the home-longing and sense of sonship might
be awakened. Let us see what we are losing
if we are living only for the world, and let us
live for Christ so truly that when we shall fall
by the scythe of death as Abner by the sword
of Joab, our fellows may sorrow for us as David
for the Son of Ner.

JASHOBEAM, AND COURAGEOUS COM-
PANIONS.

SCRIPTURE REFS.—II. *Sam.* xxiii. 15-17, and I. *Chron.* xi. 2.

T is said that King Arthur had a "round table" of the brave; but we know that David had one earlier. The poet Laureate has made the one celebrated in his "Idyls of the King," but long before Arthur lived David's had caused the deeds of his noblest followers to be recorded and recited.

This chapter and the eleventh and twelfth of the first book of Chronicles give accounts of the men who belonged to David's army who were among the "mighty men, helpers of the war,"—the men who aided in his accession to the throne. There were several divisions of these warriors, and chiefs among the captains. The leaders in this assemblage of Heroes were these three, *Jashobeam, Eleazar* and *Shammah.*

During the wars with the Philistines, David, heated with the sun while scanning the hosts of his enemies, suddenly gave expression to a desire for water from the well of Bethlehem. "Oh that one would give me drink of the water of the well of Bethlehem, which is by the gate!" He had probably been thinking *of his boyhood,* and gave utterance to this, which was a sort of passionate outburst of home longing. It was just like David with his intense nature to speak and act in the way recorded in these verses. Just as an Italian in a northern region longs for the fruits and blue skies of his own land, so David longed for this water. He contrasts its limpid freshness with the muddy liquid brought to him from the much-used well or shallow pond near his encampment.

Perhaps wearied of rule, he desired to be a boy again, and so thought of the well around which he had played. His remark was heard by the men who formed his body guard or staff, and they resolved to obtain the water for him.

What a manifestation *of devoted loyalty* is here! A hint is enough. No command had to be given. Such service could not be commanded, only prompted. Why were they so attached to David? They had shared his dangers and exile, and now his prosperity. Moreover, he had so acted as to *inspire respect* and devotion. Had not he led them skilfully? Had not he lopped off Goliath's head? Had he not outdone all who followed him? The three talked together probably of what they had done, and compared notes to the advantage of David. "I recollect," says Jashobeam, "lifting up the spear against eight hundred, whom I slew at one time." Says Eleazar, "When the rest of the army had gone, I stood and fought until my hand clave to the sword and the people returned to the spoil." Then Shammah breaks in, "And I repulsed a troop from the field of lentils ; I stood and defended it, and the Lord wrought a great victory." But all would then confess that David's victory over Goliath was greater than all. What ought they not to do for a king of such courage, and at the same time such affection. They determine that his wish for the water shall be gratified, and they plan their sortie with caution, and carry it out with courage and celerity. At dusk they steal up, break through the lines of the enemy, overpowering and silencing the sentinels, and reach the well at last. Two defend the one who draws the water, then, putting it into a skin, that one slings it over his shoulder, and they fight their way out of the surrounding host, bearing the water to the king. Brave men ! Brave act ! Loyal service !

What ought not we to venture for the sake of *our* Leader and King? What ought not we to be ready to do to gain the Water of Life? It is far better than that of the well of Bethlehem. It only can satisfy the soul ; and it will be as a "well of water springing up into eternal life." Having found this great boon, we should show our devotion to Christ in every way possible.

We should be loyal to Him who is a greater
leader than David. Men have been true to
conscience and to Christ at the peril of life, and
this should stimulate us to greater devotion
and faithfulness. Listen to old Condé, when his
king told him to choose between three things—
either to hear Mass, to go to death or imprisonment. He said, "With regard to the first, I have
fully determined never to hear it ; and as to the
second and third course, I am perfectly indifferent, and I leave the choice to your majesty."
Brave, bold words, the outcome of a true faith.
Oh, it does us good to listen to such words, and
to contemplate such devotion. Such loyalty
to truth and to Christ thrills us. We want,
all want, more of the heroic spirit. The world
wants *men*, not weaklings, and Christ and His
Church call now for such loyal, manly souls.

High appreciation of service was manifested
by David when he understood at what risk that
water had been brought. When he saw the
loyalty of his brave followers, he was overpowered with a sense of his own unworthiness, and
repentance for the expression of his *rash desire*.
He did not hesitate to admit that it was a
rashness. He felt that there was no dishonour
in recalling a mistake. How could he have been
so careless ! He blames himself severely ; but at
the same time he rejoices over the devotedness
of his chiefs or generals. He values the water
as though it had been blood :—" Is not this the
blood of men ? " He could not be indifferent to

their lives, and their blood was synonymous with
life. " He shall redeem their souls from violence,
and precious shall their blood be in His sight."
(Ps. lxxii. 14.) David will not drink—it is very
tempting; but no, he cannot bring himself to
enjoy that which had been procured at such a
cost. David pours it out before God, as the
only One who is worthy to receive so great a
sacrifice. Some might blame him for appearing
to throw a slight on the act of the brave men—
judicious waste. There is an expensive penu-
riousness and a short-sighted selfishness that
would condemn such an act; we believe, however, that it would have been selfish to drink
that water, but to pour it out was to put a value
upon it, far higher than could have been put
upon it by his drinking it. His act was not like
that of the Pasha in the Russo-Turkish war,
who, when English Doctors went to him at a
great cost, eager to help the wounded Turkish
soldiers, repulsed them, and firmly declined
their services.

Some had indignation when the woman brake
the alabaster box of ointment over Christ's feet;
but He looked at it in another light—He approved that loving, loyal, lavish "waste." So
David approved the act of his captains. Only
selfish souls could be indifferent to the lives of
others. David's piety equalled their bravery—
if they were devoted, he was devout. He would
not drink, but poured it out before the Lord.
His evident approval was sufficient to reward

them. His pouring it out on the ground spoke more forcibly than any words the lofty appreciation in which he held their brave act. So Christ's approval will at last be our great reward for anything we may have done, whether of great service or only as the expression of true devotion.

But let us not speak of what we have done, but of what has been done for us by our King. He has broken through the ranks of evil, to gain for us the Water of Life. In solid phalanx the evil powers stood around His cross, but He penetrated the dark hosts, and secured for us the Waters of Salvation. He opened the fountain also for the washing away of sin and all uncleanness. We know not the cost, because we know so little of the nature of Him who, though He was rich, for our sakes "became poor." None could measure the depth of the sufferings of the Redeemer, the anguish of soul arising not only from man's rejection and sin, but the hiding of the Father's face. But He was willing to endure all that He might effect His purpose of love and save that which was lost.

An incident has been recorded concerning that great Italian patriot who did so much towards promoting the unity of the peninsula, which shows his kindness of heart, readiness of action, and persistency of purpose, and explains, in a measure, the secret of the power he had gained over others. One evening in 1861, as the patriot was returning home, he met a Sardinian shepherd lamenting the loss of a lamb out of his flock. The soldier patriot at once turned to his staff, and announced his intention of scouring the mountain in search of the lamb. A grand expedition was immediately organised—lanterns were brought, and old officers of many a campaign started off, full of zeal, to seek for the fugitive. But no lamb was found; and the soldiers were ordered to their beds. The next morning the general's attendant found him in bed fast asleep. He was surprised at this, for the general was always up before anybody else. The attendant went off softly, and returned in half-an-hour—still the general slept. After another delay, the attendant thought he was doing his duty by awakening his master. The general rubbed his eyes, and his attendant rubbed his too when he saw the old warrior take from under the covering the lost lamb, bidding him convey it to the shepherd. The head of the forces at least had kept up the search and, when all others abandoned it, was successful. Now, what would not be the effect on the soldiers and officers of such persistency on the part of so great a man?

What ought not to be the effect of Christ's love upon us? Surely to Him we ought to give our truest gratitude and most loyal service. Christ seeks us, and values our devotion, even as David valued that of those who were numbered among his brave ones. We can be faithful and courageous; we should fight hard

7

against the temptation to postpone or to put aside the question as to whether we will serve Him thus fully or not. Break through the ranks of opposition, as Jashobeam, Eleazar, and Shammah. As Christians, we should be ready to obey our Master's slightest desire, and should stand before the Saviour consciously and absolutely consecrated, even as the three brave men were to David.

ABEL'S ORACLE;

OR PRUDENCE AND PEACEABLENESS.

SCRIPTURE REFERENCES, II. *Sam.* xx., 16-22

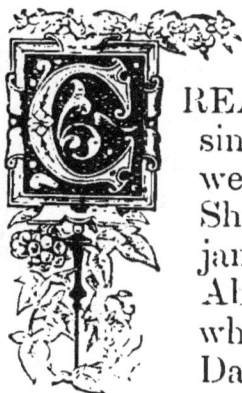

GREAT is sometimes the power of a single individual to imperil the welfare of a whole community. Sheba, the son of Bichri, a Benjamite, did this for the people of Abel. He was a characterless man, who headed a revolt in the time of David. The king was but just restored after the revolt of Absalom. The men of Judah had been foremost in effecting that restoration, and this somehow made the rest of Israel very jealous. Very bitter words were exchanged between the men of Judah and Benjamin. One man was glad to foster the bitterness, for he had personal ends to serve. He led some to say, " We have no part in David, neither have we inheritance in the son of Jesse. Every man to his tents, O Israel." Open rebellion was soon the outcome of big words. The strong arm of law and order had to be brought to bear in order

to restore peace and to quell anarchy. Rebellion
could not be permitted, for that would have
been a great wrong to the nation, hence the
commander in chief attacked rapidly, and
scattered with his quick movement and strong
blows the insurgents, pursuing the leader,
Sheba, up to the city gates of Abel of Bethmaachah.   Here he had sought shelter, because
he believed he had therein some sympathizers.
Joab's character is strongly marked out in all
this transaction.   He was "politic, decided, bold,
unscrupulous, though never needlessly cruel."
He was impulsive and even revengeful. No
life was safe that stood in his way, though
from policy he never sacrificed the most insig-
nificant life *without a purpose*. His purpose
was the general good.   He knew what great
harm this one man Sheba could do, and
he knew that he had been tolerated long
enough.   Now that he has taken refuge in an
innocent city, and thinks himself secure, Joab
is obliged to attack it with energy.   The
people at first thought it a gallant thing to
harbour and defend such a man as Sheba.
They are enamoured of his boldness in standing against such odds.   Moreover they had
some sympathy with him in his hatred of
Judah.   The traitor had found his work easy,
because people were prepared for revolt.   He
moved them to desperation, worked upon their
feelings, depicted imaginary wrongs, aroused
hatred, and led them to the verge of ruin.

The people in Abel of Bethmaachah are
on the verge of ruin now, for Joab is battering away at the walls. Soon his soldiers
will be pouring into the city, and the
sword will devour and destroy. Soon
nothing will be heard but the shrieks of
women and children, the groans of the
wounded and the cries of the dying.

Now if a man could do wrong and suffer
alone it would be more tolerable. No man
can, however, suffer alone. We always suffer in
greater or less degree by any sin committed by
our fellows. We are all so co-related, interwoven. There is such a *solidarité* existing; and
in proportion to the width of the circle of influence of any individual, so will be the evil
wrought upon others by this wrong doing, even
as it is far more damaging to an arch to take
out the *key*-stone or the corner stone, than to
remove any other portion thereof.

We may even, as one has said, "sin in the
persons of other men," for those who received
an evil influence from us may go on sinning
through that influence, and so suffer through
their own sin and ours. Even when we have
passed from this stage of existence *our influence
will still live.* "Being dead we speak," either for
evil or for good. It is so hard to check evil once
committed, much more to stop it altogether. A
sin is like a maddened horse that has slipped
from your hand, and with head lifted and
reins flying, harness broken and shafts clat-

tering, goes dashing into a crowded thoroughfare, to the imminent danger of many. We little
think of what damage we work to others by
our sins, or even by *one sin*. Sin is a *real*
and *terrible fact*. We cannot deny its existence, because we see, alas, too many evidences
of its existence around us, as well as feel
them in our own hearts. And it brings such
fearful consequences to the unsuspecting. It
is like that disease so subtle among the cattle
of France, that even a sheep grazing on grass
trodden by others diseased may receive the
deadly germ into its system and perish. So
the consequence of any sin may be terrible
to others who had not any part in the sin, and
were unexpectedly and unwittingly drawn within the circle of its evil power. There were thus
numbers in the city of Abel who had no part
in the treason of Sheba, but who were involved
in its consequences. The loyal, peaceable, and
true, the infirm and weak, women and children, were all involved, and that through one
man. Joab does not wish to injure them, but
he must reach Sheba.

Every day we meet with instances of similar
suffering. A father has forged a cheque, and his
children must suffer, although it is not their
fault that they are his children. A mother is
fretful and gloomy, and the whole household is
made wretched. A brother defrauds another, or
over-speculates with money entrusted to him,
and his sisters are ruined; or a marriage just

about to take place is checked, and the sister's hopes blighted. Sin is terrible. Its near and remote consequences are beyond our power of conception. We are all centres of some influence, and we can individually do more or less harm to others. If we could realize the amount of injury we may do by a careless word or mean act to the reputation or souls of others, we should not dare to sin.

Sheba brings hunger, disease, slavery, ignominy, and death to others. He lays the city walls low and brings a ban for disloyalty upon it, a ban from which it will never recover. What harm in a town or country *one* man can do! Evil, such as if he could but measure it, would blanch his cheek, and if he had a heart, break it. Even seizing such an one and incarcerating him or putting him to death does not check all the damage.

The deed of folly and sin soaks into the lives of others, and breaks out or flows on in channels undreamt of. It is not their own crimes only which men commit, they harrow them into the breast of another. We can do nothing that shall have an end in ourselves. "One sinner destroyeth much good." The rough, unskilled hand touching a picture, or attempting to repair the delicate mechanism of a watch, may do much greater damage than can be conceived. So one Sheba can imperil a city. So one hidden sin can endanger salvation— can ruin a soul.

But we see on the other hand, that the *power of an individual to bless may balance the evil wrought by the careless and selfish.* While Joab's soldiers are battering the walls, above the din is heard the voice of a woman—"Hear! listen! listen, I pray you! Call Joab, tell him to come hither, that I may speak with him."

By the action of the besieged, the besiegers see that the woman is to speak in their name. Moreover, they may have recognised her as the wise woman of Abel, of whom they had heard. Joab is brought, and stands flushed with effort and expectant of victory. He listens to see if the words of the woman indicate readiness to yield.

She says, "Art thou Joab?"

"I am he."

"Hear the words of thine handmaid."

Curtly he replies, "I do hear."

She begins by reminding him how the city had once had a reputation as the seat of wise counsel. She herself had adjusted many a quarrel. She speaks of how she is one of the peaceful and faithful in Israel; upbraids Joab for seeking to destroy a city that was once held in high esteem, and to "swallow up the inhabitants of the Lord."

Joab repudiates the suggestion—"Far be it from me that I should swallow up or destroy. That is not the matter or object; but Sheba has lifted up his hand against the king, even

David. Deliver him up, and I will depart
from the city."

This was the concession the wise woman
wanted, and soon Sheba's head was thrown
over the wall. Then Joab blew the trumpet
of recall, and his soldiers dropped their arms
and refrained from further attack. The city
was saved.

We may learn that as no city is safe
with a traitor in it, so *no heart is safe where
a single sin is cherished.* We must pluck out
or cut off the sin that besets or absorbs us.
As it were better that the body of Sheba
should become headless than that a whole
city should be destroyed, so it is better for us
to give up some cherished sin than to suffer
for ever. Better pluck out the right eye, and
cut off the right hand, than allow the whole
body to be cast into hell.

We should in all circumstances seek to act
in a common sense manner. Wisdom is not
merely extraordinary knowledge, but perception. This woman seemed to inherit common
sense, that most rare of all the senses. See
what *power is exerted by gentleness,* by a soft
answer or by an unassuming manner. Said a
statesman, "A soft word often turns aside wrath
and prevents the most serious wars that threaten
to devastate the world." Some are unreasonable, and take advantage of gentleness; but
words of reviling and recrimination are always
a mistake. One may as well "try to mend

broken windows by pelting them with stones."
See how Gideon acted when the Ephraimites
were enraged at him because he had not invoked
their aid against Midian. Gideon soothed them
by asking if the mere gleaning of the grapes
of Ephraim was not better than the entire
vintage of Abiezer? "Then was their anger
towards him abated, when he said that." A
great amount of mischief might be prevented
in this world, if only contending parties could
be brought to understand each other. The
wise woman used common-sense and gentleness with Joab.

There was *no sacrifice of principle in the
action of the woman or of the citizens.*
Caiaphas in after ages suggested that it was
better that Christ should die than that the
whole nation should perish. Caiaphas cared
not that Christ was innocent. Christ had
not brought the evil Sheba had. It was
better for a nation to suffer than to permit
an innocent man to be condemned. Even
general good is not to be sought by injustice
to an individual. But there was no sacrifice
of principle by the citizens when Sheba was
rejected—it was the righteous giving up of a
sinner to retribution.

The wise woman chose a *suitable time* for
ending the strife. Some good projects are
marred through being inopportune, but it was
not so in this case. The woman had done all
she could to save the city, perhaps by sugges-

tions as to its defence; but now she sees that
there can be nothing but disaster from further
resistance, and she suggests yielding. Possibly
Joab had offered before to spare the city if
Sheba had been given up. By the woman's
words, "I am one of them that are peaceable,"
it would seem that there had been previous
suggestions as to peace, but she had not been
able to get those counsels of peace accepted.
Now is her moment. She seizes it. A few
minutes, and the chance will be gone. She
acts. She appeals again to the citizens. They
listen to her now. They think she is right
now, and Sheba's head is soon sent from them to
Joab as a flag of truce.

In the book of Ecclesiastes ix, 14, it is written,
"There was a little city and few men in it,
and there came a great king against it and
besieged it, and built great bulwarks against
it. Now there was found in it a poor wise
man, and he by his wisdom delivered the
city." Here a *woman's* timely wisdom delivered
the city of Abel.

In the matter of our salvation, we would
say, let not the traitor of pride and procrastination be permitted to remain within the soul.
Cast away self-will and pride, and seek peace.
Law is terrible so long only as we are not in
harmony with it, not when our sin is forgiven.
Christ has come to make peace. He is our peace.
He saw our danger. At the right moment He
interposed. He allowed Himself to bear con-

tumely and crucifixion that we might be delivered. He took as it were the place of Sheba. He was made sin for us, and permitted Himself to be cast out, that we might be saved. He died in our place, for sin-enslaved, defiant, rebellious souls. He did it unasked. He did it from pure love. He saw not one man, but a whole world perishing, and He said, "Better that I should die than that all these should perish."

RIZPAH: OR, RELATIVE SUFFERING.

SCRIPTURE REFERENCE—II. *Sam.* xxi. 1-14.

THREE years, "year after year," famine desolated the land of Israel. The famine probably arose from the people engaging in war and neglecting agriculture. This neglect, even under a king so careful for his subjects as David, could not go on without bringing bitter consequences. Gloom and despair were spread over the whole land. David enquired as to the reason for this great suffering, and learned from the divine oracle that it was because Saul had, in his mistaken zeal for Israel, slain the Gibeonites. Disliking their incorporation with Israel, Saul had determined to have a distinct nation. Unmindful of the covenant made with them by Joshua (Josh. ix. 15), he devised means of complete extermination, but could not completely carry it out. He only wanted an excuse to cut off those he disliked. His sin slept; the debt was not only uncancelled, but the interest accumulated. He forgot, possibly, his sin before he died; but God had not forgotten it. Divine judgments always, sooner or later, overtake sin. These judgments have a long reach backward as well as forward, and time does not wear out the guilt of that or of any act.

We may generally see the cause of any suffering if we only go far enough. David began to enquire, and found out the cause. When he learned at the mouth of the priest the reason for the successive famines, he at once sent for the Gibeonites and enquired what he should do for them. They spoke of what Saul's "bloody house"—for this was the general character of his own and his family's dealings,—had done to them, and demanded a most terrible penalty. The demand of the Gibeonites was in harmony only with that crude, cruel, harsh age. They demanded that the survivors of Saul's race should be handed over to them, that they might do that which they thought would appease outraged law.

Some have supposed that David was glad of the opportunity of getting rid—after an Eastern fashion,—of possible rivals to the throne ; but this could not have been his motive, or he would not otherwise have spared the one who was the only direct and lineal descendant, Mephibosheth, the eldest son of the deceased heir apparent, Jonathan.

Two sons of Saul, children of Rizpah, and five of his grandsons were taken and slain. Suddenly they were called to give up their lives.

They were not only slain, but hanged upon a
wall on the hill of Gibeah, as being accursed.
[This was in part in accordance with what was
written in Deut. xxi. 23.] The whole event
was a terrible and dark tragedy, but under
the black thundercloud was one cheering ray
of light.

If all forsake those who hang as accursed,
Rizpah will not. She cannot hinder the seizure
of her sons and relatives, but she can watch
that no further dishonour shall be done to their
bodies. She takes sackcloth, spreads it to shield
her by day and to rest on at night. Stifled by
the heat, and chilled by the cold night air, she
remains near to those sun-scorched, haggard,
weird, blackened, dishonoured bodies, watching
to save them from further ignominy. Now
standing, now sitting, now seeming half dead
with sleepiness, and then quivering with daring
effort, with her single arm she drives away the
hungry dogs of the city, and with her voice
scares away the vultures that would soon have
devoured the dead. Alone on the weary rock,
week after week, for several months she remains, from the beginning of barley harvest,
until rain drops upon them out of heaven.
How strangers and passers-by must have gazed
with interest from a distance on that lone
watcher, and either pitied or jibed, spoken of her
as mad, or cheered her with their usual " Peace
be with you."

We may gaze with admiring wonder at a

woman's faithfulness, love, and patience. What
faith ! She believed that sooner or later God
would be entreated for the land, and that
when the rains came it would show that guilt
had been appeased, and that her dear ones
might at least have honourable burial. She believed that they hung there, not for their own
sin, but for the sin of others, and, therefore, she
does not forsake them. It is so easy to turn our
back on those whom the world forsakes. The
forsaken, if living, feel intensely their loneliness,
but even wrong-doers should not be made to
feel too bitterly their wrong, lest they should
be eaten up of overmuch sorrow.

Rizpah would not believe her sons were wrong.
How like a *woman !* They are always slowest
to believe wrong, and always readiest to bear
the heaviest burdens for those they love. And
what a burden, to watch through all those slowly
passing weeks. Think of the slow days and
long nights. Women will attend others when
man would forsake. Not only will they do it
for loved ones, but as nurses they will do it for
the needy. We have heard more than one speak
with enthusiasm of their work of watching, and
have known that they have been ready to give
their lives for others.

What a hint we have here of *the sorrows that
are silently endured.* In thousands of homes
every day, there are wives and sisters and daughters who are watching as assiduously, either by
the bedside of loved sufferers, or mourning at

their death, as Rizpah on the rock of Gibeah. How many there are out of whose lives all that is bright is gone, because one to whom they gave their heart's best devotion is lying pulseless, in the blank stare of death. To them it seems strange that others should be able to smile when they have so great reason to weep, or to attend to minor affairs while they have one great over-shadowing trouble. And how many have stood at the graveside, and then gone back to the silence of the home only to think of all joyous associations as being for ever broken so far as this life is concerned. They feel how impotent is their keen sorrow and wild love to restore the belov-ed dead. Nothing now can send a single thrill of joy to their crushed hearts; nothing can undo wrongs done to the departed; nothing can atone for words of harshness and acts of unkindness. They sit and sigh for "the touch of the vanished hand, and the sound of a voice that is still." Silently, like Rizpah, and alas ! often hopelessly, they have to bear their sorrow.

And we learn how some of the *bitterest trials of life come through the wrongdoings of others.* Rizpah had nothing to do with Saul's sin, and yet she had to bear some of the fearful conse-quences. And many a son or daughter has to suffer for the mistake of a parent, and parents have bitterly to sorrow over the waywardness of their children.

Here, too, we see how Christ has suffered through the sin of others. There was *no* sin in

8

Him. Yet was He treated as a sinner, because He became one with us. Love bound Him to us. He was willing to stand by us. He saw us dead and came and became as one dead that He might save us. How He drove back the vultures of sin and the demons of darkness! How He hung on the cross in the full blaze of a broken law that He might take away the sin of the world! How He has waited since, like Rizpah, at the door of the heart, to give life and peace, and to let the rain of His mercy drop on us out of heaven! Our sins nailed Him to the tree, but He does not love us the less. He knows that when we see how He has loved us, love will break or melt our hearts. For that sign of penitence and love He waits through the long years, as Rizpah did through days of furnace heat and nights of intensest cold, for the sign of coming rain from heaven. Oh, how unwearied is Jesus in His waiting for souls! How long He waits, until His locks are wet with the dews of heaven, and His form withered as by the solar heat! What does not Jesus bear through our indifference, our hardness, our dullness, and our sinful selfishness!

We cannot realize it. If we did, we must turn to Him. Wonder of wonders is it that He should care for us who have brought, as yet, only sorrow to Him! Why does He care for us? Why will He not cast us off? This is the one thing that amazes us as we stand beneath His cross. "Greater love hath no man than this, that he lay down his life for his friends."

The overwhelming influence of a devoted life is seen in this act of Rizpah. That silent, watching woman little thought how others were taking note of her,— how her heroic action would be recorded in the Book which would be the most widely read of all books,— how others would talk of her, not only in the fields and streets, but in the court, and to the king himself. David was told of what she had done, and he will not be outdone in thoughtfulness by that woman. The rains have come. Wrong-doing is atoned for. Hence the king gives the command to remove the bodies and give them the burial of a king's sons.

Example has immense power. Men submit to it more readily than to any commands. Of it speaks Hudibras—

> " Example, that imperious dictator
> Of all that's good or bad to human nature ;
> By it the world's corrupted or reclaimed,
> Hopes to be saved or studies to be damned."

However obscure, we cannot be sure but that our example may have a good or an evil influence. In proportion to the extent of our circle, so our power for good or evil.

Rizpah was related to the past monarch of Israel, and had an influence wider than she thought. David was struck at once with the devotion of the woman, and was led by that to command that which was right to be done to the dead. So may we be led to be more self-sacrificing by the example of all the good and of Christ. May we be fired by His example, and saved by His sacrifice ! Let us come under the overwhelming influence of that devoted life.

Faithful love is finally rewarded. Rizpah, at last, when the dead are buried, can rest, and only think with a shudder of the long and weary days when her strong arm drove off the vultures, or of the nights when the wild beasts were only kept at bay by the fire that flashed from her eye, and the force that she threw into her voice. She had saved the forms of her loved ones from desecration, and they had at last had honourable burial. In that is her reward. And as we think of Him who was homeless, rejected, crucified, we ask, Will not Christ see of the travail of His soul and be satisfied ? We cannot understand the depth of that travail : His long nights of prayer : His watchings on mountain top and in the valley garden : His endurance of the hardness of opponents and the unfaithfulness of friends ! We know it was severe. For all that He endured He will have His rich reward.

Be sure also, O toilers for Christ and watchers for souls, that you will share whatever reward Christ has. " To sit with Him on His throne " means that He will share His honour with His faithful ones.

Every devout watching Rizpah and every sorrowing soul shall also have not only at last a full reward, but shall see that God has been an unseen sympathizer and helper in every bitter trial and desolate grief.

UZZAH; OR THE DANGER OF FAMILIARITY WITH SACRED THINGS.

Scripture Reference—II *Sam.* vi. 6, 7.

THE ark was the most sacred possession of the Israelites. Minute directions had been divinely given
in respect to its construction, position, portage, and preservation. In
it had been laid up mementoes of
Divine interposition,—the tables of
the law, the incorruptible manna,
and the budding rod of Aaron.
Upon it during the journeys of the Israelites
through the desert, the pillar of cloud and fire
had rested, and when it was stationary at Shiloh
the Shekinah light shone over it. The ark was
the sign of the covenant existing between God
and Israel. It was called "the ark of God," and
was the place of the mercy-seat. Even the
enemies of Israel spoke of it with reverence and
dread. When God for the sin of Israel allowed
it to be taken by the Philistines, the wife of
Phinehas named her child with bitter sorrow

and dying breath, Ichabod, because the glory was departed from Israel.

God would not allow the Israelites to trust in the ark instead of in Himself. When they, presuming on their safety on account of its possession, bore it into the battle-field, God allowed it to be taken and carried into the land of the Philistines. Although these foes of God's people rejoiced when they gained possession of that which hitherto had been a defence to Israel, they were soon glad to be rid of it. Numerous painful visitations made even the idolatrous priests of Dagon come to the conclusion that the ark of God ought to be sent back to Israel. They determined to send it back, but they knew not of any special directions as to the method of transport, and therefore sent it back in a new cart drawn by milch kine. Seven months it had been outside the borders of Israel. When it came back the men of Bethshemesh received it, but because of a calamity following on their irreverent curiosity, it was handed over to the inhabitants of Kirjath-jearim. Abinadab, a Levite, received it, and consecrated his son Eleazar to the exclusive care of it. In Kirjath-jearim it remained seventy years,—all through the period of Samuel's judgeship, Saul's kingship, and David's struggles. When Saul was dead and David established in the kingdom, then the son of Jesse thought it would be better to have the ark nearer to himself, and arranged for its removal.

The removal was begun with great joy. A

new cart was prepared, and in this the ark was placed. A procession was formed, and with music and shouting the ark was moved from its seventy years' resting-place. All went well for a time. David seemed more joyous than all others. Suddenly his joy was checked. They arrived at the threshing-floor of one Nachon, where doubtless the ruts made by the passage of the oxen and carts were deep. Here the oxen that drew the cart along stumbled, and the ark was jolted about and almost precipitated into the mire. Uzzah, who had undertaken to watch the ark while his brother Ahio drove the oxen, put forth his hand to save it from falling. That touch was death. We are told that "God smote him there for his error, and there he died by the ark of God" (2 Sam. vi. 7).

Now this is not a very inviting subject, but it is one full of instruction.

Some would have us believe that this was an accident; that Uzzah, in the effort to save the ark, dislocated his shoulder, or broke his arm, and died of hæmorrhage. We are told, however, that it was a Divine judgment. David so understood it, and "he was displeased." Sadly he gazed on the pallid corpse of Uzzah, and trem- blingly thought of the danger to himself. When one apparently so good as Uzzah was not spared, how shall he avoid like judgment?

Now God intended by this terrible visitation to teach a lesson of great importance. It is one that needs to be uttered even at this day with emphasis, viz., *the need that exists for the deepest reverence in all things connected with the Divine service, and the danger that arises from over-familiarity with sacred things.*

Uzzah was a Levite, and he knew or ought to have known the commands of God with respect to the ark. In Numb. iv. 15, it is written that those who had to bear the ark were "not to touch any holy thing, lest they die." Not only so, but the ark was to be *covered*, and so kept from the gaze of the irreverent. This had been neglected. Again, that which was to be *borne only on men's shoulders* was put on a cart. This was a gross piece of neglect. If the Philistines from ignorance put it on a cart, the Israelites were not thereby justified in breaking a command and following the lead of the idolatrous. That which was tolerated in Philistines would not be allowed in Israel. God even approved the act of the Philistines, for He caused the milch kine to forego their instincts and go away from their calves fastened up at home, that they might drag the ark to the borders of Israel ; but He could not approve the neglect of Israelites who knew, and should have observed, the Divine will.

Then it is probable that the offence of Uzzah was aggravated by the fact that he had not sufficient reverence for the Divine command. The ark had been for seventy years under the care of his father and family. Eleazar, who had been set apart to take care of it, was probably dead. It may be that neither Uzzah nor Ahio his brother had ever thought that it was important that they should be consecrated to the work. They, presuming on their Levitical descent, may have taken upon themselves informally the position of attendants. Constant familiarity with it may have led them to think of it with even somewhat of contempt. It was like a piece of useless furniture. They may have forgotten how interwoven that ark was with religious and national life. To them it may have seemed a sort of Nehushtan. Others regarded it with expectancy and reverence, but to them it was only so much wood and gold. And thus many regarded Christ's cross as so much wood, and His death as a martyrdom, forgetting that they are of infinite value as the sign and seal of the expiation of sin and salvation of the world. There was no virtue in the ark, any more than in the cross itself, apart from God's appointment. God's revealed will makes all the difference in respect to any act or observance. That was a ceremonialistic age. Men were under the tutelage of these things, and until the time for their entrance on the freedom of the gospel was come, none had any authority to set aside or trifle with a divine injunction. Doubtless Uzzah had touched the ark in an over-familiar way before, and it may have been passed over; now he does it publicly, and as evil would result from his example, judgment follows.

We find a similar judgment fell on a man who

went out to gather sticks on the Sabbath ; and
on the men of Bethshemesh, to whom the ark
first came. They opened it and looked in,—
probably seeking greedily gold supposed to be
hidden there ; or from curiosity to see what the
Philistines had done to it—and Divine displeasure was manifested. Seventy of them were
smitten out of the fifty thousand of that district
(*vide* " Speaker's Commentary " on 1 Sam. vi. 19,
20). Here it was a severe visitation, because
as Bethshemesh was a city of priests, they
should have been more careful to observe the
Divine commands. There is always a propor-
tionate punishment inflicted for privilege and
office abused.

Some would say, " But how trifling the sin,
compared with the severity of the punishment."
Sin is never a trifle. Disobedience to God is not
a trifle. Peter's few words of denial were easily
spoken, but they were no trifle in their consequences. A few drops of prussic acid taken into
the system are trifling so far as size and substance are concerned, but not as to results. To
touch the ark irreverently was no trifle ; it
indicated a state of heart not in accord with the
office filled.

Besides, the attention of the people had to
be arrested, and the need for reverence em-
phasized. Hence the sin was not passed by.
Great benefit arose. As in the case of the men
of Bethshemesh, the exclamation was raised,
" Who is able to stand before the Lord ? " so

here we find David saying, "How shall the ark of God come to me?" A deep impression of the need for purity on their part and of unswerving justice on God's part was made.

Uzzah sinned with his eyes open. He knew the commands. He sinned with the warning of Bethshemesh before him. He sinned publicly, and he perished suddenly and miserably. It was a sudden and severe judgment, but that was a stern age, and the people could only be influenced by such means. David saw the reason for the visitation, and so when he summoned courage to move on instead of going up to Jerusalem he turned aside to Obed-edom the Gittite, one who was not only a Levite but probably a Kohathite, to whom it rightly pertained to bear the ark. We find in Joshua xxi. 24, that Gath-rimmon was not only one of the Levitical cities, but that it belonged to the special section of the Kohathites, whose duty it was to bear the ark. Hence we infer that Obed-edom was one of the Kohathites. Further, when David again essayed to bring it to Jerusalem, we find that it was *not* again subject to the dishonour of being put in a cart, but was borne on men's shoulders, and Obed-edom was one of those who took part in the ceremony (1 Chron. xv. 15—21).

It may be objected that the punishment was needlessly severe, in that Uzzah's *intentions were good.* This is very plausible; but good intentions do not always justify wrong-doing. Many have been led astray by this sophistry. We may not do evil that good may come. God will not have His laws broken under pretence of serving Him. We may not bend to a course of expediency under the pretext of glorifying God. Whatever is really wrong must not be permitted, and it was wrong for Uzzah to break the Divine command and thereby perhaps lead others to similar irreverence.

Uzzah died by the side of the ark of God. How terrible! Yet what a warning for the ages! Being engaged in religious services or connected with sacred things cannot ensure salvation. Spiritual death is the outcome of presumption, even though there be some manifestation of religious zeal. We should, therefore, watch any tendency to levity or lightness in Divine worship, or in treatment of sacred subjects. To use Scripture to point a witticism or to regard the Divine book as an ordinary book is not a good sign. There should be no listlessness in worship or in listening to God's truth. Is not such carelessness an indication of indifference to the presence of that divine Spirit in which we believe? Can we be cold and heartless in the presence of the King of Heaven? Can we even go up to God's house only as a matter of duty, or keep up our outward observance of religion merely to maintain a claim to respectability? The manner of our entering on worship is not unimportant. The Jew was accustomed to go up to the temple hastily, in order to show his love for the habitation of God, and he went away as slowly as possible, to indicate his regret at leaving the place " where His honour dwelleth." Christians might well learn a lesson in this respect.

Now this subject may not seem so important as some others, but it is no slight thing to remove from minds difficulties that spring up in reading such a circumstance as this breach on Uzzah, or the visitation at Bethshemesh. The lessons conveyed are also salutary. They are beneficial to all Christians, and especially to those who have to teach or pray or preach. Those who have to engage in sacred services know how great is the temptation, arising from the frequency of engagement or familiarity with sacred things, to lose that profound sense of their significance which it is of the highest importance to maintain. Perfunctory performance of worship is a mockery to heaven. God says, " Who hath required this of your hands? Bring no more vain oblations." " Be ye clean that bear the vessels of the Lord." Ministers feel that they have to watch and pray lest in any sense the sin of Uzzah should become theirs. And every man has need to pray, " Keep back thy servant also from presumptuous sins ; let them not have dominion over me." Sins of ignorance are often condoned, but sins of presumption are sure to bring a terrible retribution. Sins of presumption are generally the outcome of sins secretly indulged. The moral sense gets so dulled that we soon yield to something far worse. Belshazzar afterwards, like Uzzah, put forth his hand to touch holy things, and praised the false gods of Babylon by drinking wine to them in the sacred vessels brought from Jerusalem. In that same hour came forth the mystic hand that wrote on the palace plaster the divine condemnation; and "that same night was Belshazzar the king of the Chaldeans slain."

Now this subject has a very pertinent reference to those who come to God's house over and over again, who hear but heed not, who praise with the lips but whose hearts are far from God. They think they may go on as they like in life, and change when they like. Meanwhile the very promises of the gospel only petrify by frequent hearing without acceptance, and the attitude of the soul becomes fixed in antipathy to the claims of Christ by the repeated rejection of Divine mercy. When such die they seem like Uzzah to perish close "by the ark."

There was one who stretched out her hand to touch the hem of Christ's garment, but no irreverence was in her touch, but only faith and hope. It was effective. It delighted Christ. "Somebody hath touched Me," He said, "virtue had gone" out of Him. As speedily as death came as the retribution for Uzzah's irreverent touch, healing and life came to that woman. She through that touch rose up strong, forgiven, hopeful, grateful before Christ; but Uzzah through his touch perished close "by the ark."

THE WIFE OF THE KENITE; OR TRUST AND TREACHERY.

SCRIPTURE REFERENCE—*Judges* iv. 18-24. v. 24-31.

HE people chosen by God in the furnace of Egypt, and led by Him through the wilderness, had turned aside from Him, and gave themselves up to evil. To rebuke them the Lord allowed them to be brought under the tyranny of an alien power. Jabin was permitted to subdue them. He struck terror into the hearts of the enfeebled Israelites by his nine hundred chariots of iron, and harried them by the hand of a great commander of his hosts, Sisera. "Twenty years he mightily oppressed the children of Israel." The wife of Lapidoth,—Deborah, a prophetess,— one to whom all Israel came for decision in difficult cases, felt this oppression most keenly. As she listened under the palm tree—her court —to the tales of sorrow and injustice, her soul was stirred within her. She looked around for some one who should help at such a time.

Barak of Kedesh-Naphtali seemed to her to
be the only one fitted to lead a revolt. She
sent for him, and he came at her summons,
but declined to head the revolt unless she
would go with him. To this she consented,
but she told Barak at the same time that
he should not have altogether the honour of
delivering the people, but that the Lord would
give Sisera into the hand of a woman.

One woman began this campaign, and another gave to it the final stroke of victory.
Because Deborah prophesied of this grand
result, and because she praised Jael as
"blessed above women," it has been supposed
that all that was done by Jael had the
Divine approval. Certainly the action of Jael
is recorded as if it were worthy to be praised,
and therefore considerable and real difficulty
surrounds the subject in many minds.

The battle went against the Canaanites.
They were discomfited before the Israelites.
Such was the slaughter, that it seemed that
all the chariot-aided host were only as grass
falling before the scythe-like sweep of Israel's
sword. Sisera, the mighty warrior, was over-
whelmed, and himself had to seek safety in
flight. His charioteer drove most furiously,
but the horses could not go swiftly enough
for the defeated and terrified general. He
knew that he was too easy a mark for the
pursuing Israelites, and that their swiftest
runners would hunt for him. Hence, slipping

down behind his chariot, he left it to go on its way, and by its wheel-marks to delude the enemy into pursuing a wrong route. While it dashed along in one direction he sped away in another, to take shelter among those whom he believed to be friendly towards his nation. He came towards the camp of the Kenite. Jael, the wife of Heber the sheik, had been most anxious to know how the battle had gone, and descrying Sisera approach, went to meet him. " Turn in, my lord," she said, " turn in to me; fear not." Affrighted and weary, he was nothing loath to rest. He entered the tent, and she, giving first milk in place of the water for which he asked, wrapped him in a mantle to hide him until he should sleep. She listened tremblingly to the heavy breathings of the wearied warrior. As the sound stole through the tent-folds she knew that he was soundly asleep. Taking a tent-peg and a mallet, she stepped softly within. For a moment or two she gazes with hatred on the prostrate form, then, nerving herself to the deed, she lifts the hammer, and strikes the tent-peg through his temples. His struggles were brief. Soon all was silence. She had killed and fastened at one fell blow the Canaanite general to the ground.

This is in brief the account. How are we to judge of it? Is it written down as approved of God? Not necessarily. It is put into the narrative as a matter of *historical interest, and as being connected with the welfare of Israel.* It is not essential that we should think of it as Divinely approved, any more than we think of the rash vow of Jephthah, or the vagaries of Samson or of Saul, as approved by God. When Deborah speaks with exultation of the act, we must remember that she only speaks *in harmony with the ideas of her age.*

Though a prophetess, she had but limited and local light. Christ had not come and given full light. We must avoid, therefore, measuring the character of an Old Testament saint by the standard of the New. The ethics of the Christian dispensation differ widely from those of the Mosaic. The "but I say unto you" of Christ is the reversal in great part of Mosaic morality. As also the clearer light of this age is the result of Christ's teaching, we must not judge Jael's act by present standards.

There are several things connected with the triumph of Jael which we cannot view with approval.

1. Her *falsity of word.* She told him not to fear. She deceived him by her show of kindness—giving milk instead of water, and giving it in a "lordly dish," such as would befit his distinguished rank. She deluded him into imagining that he had found a place of safety in her tent. She led him to feel secure in the attention shown by her spreading over him a mantle. The wearied warrior,

unsuspicious of treachery, had therefore yielded
to the balmy breathings of sleep. Her words
and movements were deceptive. We must
not approve them, or think that the kingdom
of God can be advanced by falsity.

2. The *breach of a covenant* was certainly
very wrong. The tribe of her husband was
under a covenant of peace with the nation
of Canaan. Treaty rights ought always to
be respected until lawfully set aside. Jael
ignored the covenant of peace when she put
the treacherous tent-peg to the temples of
Sisera. She saw that the power of Jabin was
broken, and that the interests of her tribe
would be best served by an alliance with
Israel. Hence her treachery. We are not
called upon to approve this any more than
we are the act of Judas who betrayed Christ,
or of the soldiers who nailed Him to the tree.
We know that unless Christ had died the
world's atonement must have remained un-
offered ; but then neither Judas nor the soldiers
had any such intention in their act to qualify its
enormity. To this day, those who seek shelter in the tent of the mother of the tribe,
—the wife of the sheik,—are secure for a
time. That tent is the sanctuary and refuge
of those in trouble. Knowing this, as well as
the fact of the covenant of peace between
Heber's tribe and his nation, Sisera implicitly
trusted Jael. She betrayed his trust.

Some imagine that Jael acted by Divine

inspiration. No such inspiration is, however, claimed for her by the sacred narrative. Certainly it would not be in harmony with our ideas of the Divine nature to imagine that God could put into the heart of any one a conception at once so false, so delusive, and so treacherous. Sisera, if an enemy, trusted Jael; and she, being a supposed friend, was the more treacherous.

There are, nevertheless, *certain qualities in the act of Jael that we may approve.* These qualities may help us to understand why such a glaring breach of the law of hospitality, such an act of treachery, was spoken of with such exultation. When we judge any act, we must take into account the motives which prompted it. If Jael's act had been inspired by a desire to possess herself of the jewelled girdle, or the massive helmet of the fugitive commander, her act would have been simply a murder. There was, however, no such motive. It is probable that her sympathies had been stirred towards the Israelites so "mightily oppressed" by Sisera. His cruelty brought a terrible humiliation and retribution. He, the proud warrior, to die by the hand of a despised woman! Thus tyranny calls forth treachery, and oppression raises untameable passion. Revenge is sure to be sought by the outraged and oppressed.

It was not of herself that Jael was thinking when she conceived the idea of ridding a people, to whom she was so closely related, of such an enemy. First, Jael had *faith*. She believed that Israel was under Divine care, and she wished her lot to be cast in with the chosen people. She was half a Jewess. She had more faith in God's promise than in Jabin's nine hundred chariots. Again, Jael was animated with *zeal* for God. Jael also was *bold* in her design. It required no little daring to attempt to slay such a warrior. What if her hand were too weak to drive home the tent-peg! What if he should suddenly arise, and with one blow of his mailed hand, or stroke from his sword, end her life! She was but a woman. What daring, however, she had! Women have often done deeds of daring that have equalled the loftiest reaches of manly valour. Rizpah watched through dreary weeks the bodies of her sons, enduring the inclemency of the weather, and driving off the wild beasts that came to devour. Deborah led an army, and Jael slew a Sisera. For those they love, women will dare anything. If a child or husband is in danger, what can keep them back from rushing to help or save? When Christ was forsaken by men, women clustered round His cross. When the sabbath of restraint was past and the day of resurrection dawning,—even while it was yet dark, first to the tomb came women. Yes, women can be brave, and that even in a narrow sphere. That which Jael wrought was a great deed. She might with pride stand and await the arrival of Israel's chief,

Barak, and say to him, "Come, I will show thee the man whom thou seekest." The word of prophecy was fulfilled by Jael's bravery.

That which perhaps gave to her act greater importance was the *contrast* it presented to the half-heartedness of others. The indifference of Meroz and Reuben was a matter of great regret to Deborah. At first the Reubenites promised great things; but they soon began to think of the danger to their flocks and herds should a war break out. "For the divisions of Reuben there were great searchings of heart," said Deborah afterwards, when victory was perched on Israel's banners. Bitterly Meroz was cursed for witholding help, and with equal energy Jael was praised for her bold deed. From her nothing was expected, but she did much.

It must also be admitted that the work Jael performed, although so faulty in its morality, was *useful to God's people.* Much that we may do may be helpful to God's cause, although to ourselves there will be no advantage, should the motive not be pure. Let us not work evil that God may overrule it for good. Let us, however, have energy, faith, and zeal in whatever we undertake. Anyhow, we may learn this lesson from Jael's act. Individually, let us, with respect to evils that are around and within us, boldly, unhesitatingly strike them to the ground, and hold them there. Many a soul is unhappily held captive by various evils, as firmly as Sisera by the treacherous tent-peg. Pride, overweening confidence in self, habits of self-indulgence, procrastination, and unbelief may all be as the deadly tent-peg, struck through the temple. Slowly but surely they have been driven into our natures, and we find ourselves powerless to escape. Sisera might blame a Jael for his hindrance, we have to blame ourselves.

ABIJAH; OR, EARLY PIETY & EVIL PARENTAGE.

SCRIPTURE REFERENCE—1 *Kings* xiv. 13.

A N unscrupulous, idolatrous, and wicked man was Jeroboam, the bold leader of a revolution; yet he had a soft side to his nature—love for his child. His love and his hopes were centred in Abijah. Jeroboam earnestly desired that Abijah should succeed him in the throne he had recently established by violence. The dynasty of Jeroboam was likely to suffer if this eldest and best son should die. The guilty son of Nebat becomes very anxious about his son Abijah. "That misgotten crown" of his could not keep his head from aching. What shall he do? Faith in his own idols and priests he has none. False prophets by the hundred are waiting around, willing to prophesy to their king smooth things; but Jeroboam in the hour of his sorrow despises them. To whom shall he have recourse? He bethinks himself of the man who prophesied that he would become king, and whose word had not failed, Ahijah. Although he had forsaken God, Jeroboam now in his straits sends to Jehovah's servant. It is no uncommon thing for men to act thus inconsistently and to trust more to the human agent than to the Creator. The king is in a difficult position. If it should be known that he had sent to the prophet of Jehovah, the men whom he had instituted as priests would murmur, and the people who had followed his idolatrous lead would be likely to go back from him. They, like himself, might turn from sham deities to the true God. Not only so, but he knows that he deserves reproof for his sin, and fears that he will receive it. He shrinks in a cowardly spirit from meeting God's prophet, but he hits upon an expedient which he trusts will avoid the consequences he dreads, and yet gain the advantage he desires. He persuades his wife to put off her robes and disguise herself as a poor peasant woman, to take even a meagre present of a "little bread, a few cracknels, and a little honey" to the prophet. She is to pretend that she cannot afford more. She is to cozen the prophet of God into a cheap consultation as well as a secret one. Jeroboam thinks his shallow artifice will deceive the prophet, although he expects from him a revelation of life and death. Such again is the inconsistency of worldly ideas of sacred things. The deceit, however, is soon exposed. Scarcely has Jeroboam's wife come up to the door of the prophet, than he who had only just heard the sound of her feet surprises her by the mention of her name. "Come in, thou wife of Jeroboam; why feignest thou thyself to be another?" Surprised, rebuked, and alarmed, she enters. From the prophet she hears words that cause her heart to sink within her, and she will have to take back to that hardened sinner her husband "heavy tidings."

The rebuke for ingratitude and waywardness is followed by the announcement of the most terrible judgments. The mother-messenger learns that she is not to have that saddest of all pleasures—the privilege of tending in his dying agonies the son she loves. She may not even catch his last utterance ere he passes into the world of spirits; for when she enters the city the child is to die. The sound of her own footsteps is to be his funeral knell.

The judgment on Jeroboam is this, that evil is to attend his dynasty, and that every male descendant is to die a violent death, becoming food for vultures and dogs. But with such a terrible announcement of judgment on the parent are blended mercy and consideration for the dying son. He is to come to the grave in peace, and to have what every Israelite desired —honourable burial. This was because, although belonging to the "house of Jeroboam," "in him was found some good thing towards the Lord God of Israel."

Abijah was the good son of a bad father. His name meant "Jehovah is his father." This name had probably been given before Jeroboam broke away from the service of Jehovah. The name and the character of the youth agreed. Abijah was possessed of *real* piety. To have religion is to possess the best thing possible. It is called a "good thing." Similar descriptions of religion are given in other parts of Scripture. "That good thing which was committed to thee, keep." Again, "Being confident that He who hath begun a *good work* in you will carry it on till the day of Christ." "It is a good thing that the heart be established with grace." "Mary hath chosen that *good part* that shall not be taken away." So in Abijah's heart was found "some good thing," something which had not been quenched by the idolatry and worldliness around, but which might yet burn brightly to the glory of God.

Religion is, undoubtedly, a "good thing," in that it draws man near to God, leads to good actions, gives good aims. It has a good influence on a man's companions, on the family, and on society. It is the one "good thing" for which man was created : which he had lost, but finds again in finding Christ.

The possession of a real piety by Abijah brought him *honour from men.* He had found a deep place in the affections of the people. When he died all Israel mourned for him. Men would not have cared so much for him if he had been an indifferent, callous, wilful, cruel, passionate, self-indulgent youth. Oh, if there is anything painful to look upon it is a child or youth, selfish, hard, self-willed, disobedient, sinister, careless, untruthful, idle, irreverent, in short, irreligious, loving pleasure more than proficiency in good things, and Sabbath-breaking rather than Sabbath-keeping. Where there is a different spirit men know how to appreciate it. They augur well from evidences of early love for divine things, and they are willing to help to develop the powers, and advance in knowledge, of those who show that there is some good thing in the heart. God, as well as man, honoured this early piety in Abijah. The great Father had noticed it; His prophet speaks of it. Although Abijah had such a bad father, alone of all the house of Jeroboam he was to come to the grave in peace, and have a nation's tears wept over him.

Christians should be earnest in seeking to lead others to *early* decision for Christ, remembering that youth is the most suitable because the most impressionable time. Habits of good then formed may choke the weeds of evil. Habits of evil allowed to get a start will strike their roots deeply, and scatter their seeds widely, doing damage that can never be checked. Religion is the best check to the weeds of evil, and it cannot be implanted too soon in the heart.

There are those who fear that those who come in youth to a decision for Christ are likely to wander off when they become adults. There are those who are even doubtful of the advisability of filling youthful minds with scriptural and doctrinal knowledge. We have heard even intelligent men advocate the method of leaving young people perfectly unbiased, so that they may chose what way, opinions, doctrines, church they like when they grow up. Some object to giving young people strong opinions on subjects of great difficulty, because they will find it afterwards so hard to escape from such opinions. But we have no such fear. When those who have been trained in scriptural knowledge attain to mature age they will not cherish opinions if they do not find a rational ground for their retention. Moreover, the mind cannot be kept in an equal poise. Erroneous opinions will be absorbed if good ones are not presented. A great crop of weeds will have to be tolerated if there is no harvest of worth to reap.

As well forbear to teach the alphabet, or figures, or principles of science, or the customs of trade until manhood is reached, as forbear to instil in youth the principles of morality and the doctrines of Christ—doctrines which are the embodiment of the highest morality. No; these are flimsy objections. They are out of harmony with the Divine will and revelation.

See how the Israelites were directed to teach their children—"Thou shalt talk of them when thou sittest in thine house, when thou walkest by the way, when thou liest down, and when thou risest up."

See how the best servants of God have often been found among those early taught to love

and serve Him. Joseph early sought God.
" Joshua, the son of Nun, a young man, departed
not out of the tabernacle." Obadiah from his
youth "feared the Lord." Timothy knew the
Scriptures "from a child." Josiah while yet
young "sought the God of his fathers;" and
Abijah is said early to have had "some good
thing" in his heart towards God.

Abijah became pious none too soon. He died
early. " Briers and thorns wither not so soon
as lilies and roses." Anyhow Abijah was
prepared to pass away, prepared to meet death.
He had "some good thing" in him that would
save him from perishing. He had that which,
if Christ had been then revealed, would have
found its fitting object in the Saviour.

It is well that all should be religious. It is
delightful to see those who are veterans in age
possessors of grace ; but it is still more satisfactory when we see those who are starting in
life possessing this "good thing." They may
be, by it, preserved from many a danger. Young
people know not the terrible nature of the evils
to which they are or will be sooner or later exposed. They are often ignorant of the strength
of the desires and passions in their own natures, and they often over estimate their own
ability to resist temptation. The ocean seems
so smooth to them, that they feel sure they can
steer their bark across it. They foresee no storm
they will not be able to outride, and dread no rocks
sharp enough to wreck their vessel. They are

also ignorant of the ways of the world. Sometimes guileless and unsuspicious themselves, they imagine they may trust all who come to them with smooth face and honied words. They are in danger also of imitating their elders in any sinful course of pleasure they may witness; in danger too lest irreverence and indifference should grow upon them, so that they may cease to be impressed with the importance of spiritual things when presented to them. Dangers arise to them from the worldliness and covetousness which will certainly enfold them as a fog the marshes, or as clouds the mountain top. Carelessness about the future may come. They will seize present joys at the risk of future safety. They will walk along the dizzy edge of the great precipice, look over the beetling cliff of ruin and fancy themselves secure, smile at the ruin which has overtaken others, and boast that they are able to take care of themselves. Add to these things the repudiation of advice so common to youth, and the danger of passing beyond that point whence return is impossible or resistance hopeless, and we can see how valuable is that "good thing" in the heart that saves and elevates. In Abijah there was that "good thing" which, had he lived, would doubtless have preserved him from these terrible dangers.

What a strong contrast is presented in the state of Abijah and of his father Jeroboam. The child is travelling to bliss, his parent to woe; the son has some good thing in him, but the father teaches Israel to sin and remains the upholder of idolatry. The son is wept for by all Israel, but the name of Jeroboam the son of Nebat, who pre-eminently "taught Israel to sin," is spoken of repeatedly with execration. Jeroboam dies hopeless, but Abijah finds his way to the presence of his God. What a gulf widens between the good son and his bad father!

Minor Lights of Scripture.

VASHTI, THE DIVORCED, NOT DISGRACED.

Scripture Reference—*Esther* i. 19.

AHASUERUS, the Persian monarch, yielded to the allurements of the cup, and acted foolishly. Under its influence he gave way to the desire to exhibit the beauty of his wife and queen to a miscellaneous crowd. He had shown all that he possessed. Anything and everything that could call forth further admiration from his numerous guests had been laid under tribute. At length the king has to ask himself what more he has that can yet again constrain, by its exhibition, approval and praise. The festivities are closing, and he must not linger if he would extort more flattery and adulation.

The king remembers one most precious possession, on which the eyes of his eunuchs and himself only had rested—his Sultana. He is proud of her in somewhat the same sense as

that in which a man might, at this day, be
proud of having on his wall the finest painting,
in his cabinet the rarest jewel, or in his stables
the best horse in the country.   Had there been
in him any deep affection for Vashti, he never
could have treated her after the fashion recorded.
She was to him but a toy, a harem ornament—
a slave for whom a goodly price had been paid
from out his coffers ; and shall he not, if he
choose, exhibit her ?   He wishes to send his
guests away in the best humour, and therefore
resolves to do them the greatest honour—they
shall look upon his queen.

Accustomed to have his slightest wish immediately gratified, Ahasuerus orders his chamberlains to bring Vashti with the crown royal on
her head, and set her before the people.   Probably he flatters himself that even Vashti will
be pleased to be thus honoured.

Impatiently the king awaits the arrival of
Vashti.   Little dreams he of a rebuff.   Excited
as he is at the close of the festivities, and elated,
both by the praise he has received and the wine
he has drunk, he is in no mood to brook any
opposition to his will, or even delay in carrying
out his desires.

At length the troop of chamberlains reappears.
The king looks up from his cups.   " What, and
is not the queen coming ?"   He soon hears the
explanation of her absence.   Bowing low, and in
the hesitating tones of one who has a disagreeable
task to perform, the chief chamberlain announces

"that the queen refuseth to come at the king's commandment."

"She refuseth to come! Surely my ears deceive me. Refuseth to come! What, a woman disobey me!"

How in a moment is overcast the face hitherto so complacent, the throne of dignity and majesty. A lowering, threatening scowl sits on the king's brow. More swift than any hurricane that ever swept over doomed and unsuspecting voyagers is the storm of anger that now sweeps over the countenance of Ahasuerus. And what a Vesuvius rages in his breast! A *mere woman* to cross him! All his glory, power, and majesty to be by that one woman checked. Most annoying of all, the thought that this refusal of the queen is known to the princes and nobles. They will say, "He cannot bear rule in his own house, and how shall he govern the dominion of Persia?" The king could better endure the obstinate conduct of the queen were it known only to himself. To have his domestic affairs, however, known abroad; to be the common subject of conversation and condemnation; to be the gossip of the inmates of every harem from one end of his empire to the other; to be the butt of ridicule in every bazaar of the East—this is unbearable. "The king was very wroth, and his anger burned in him."

Those around watch the king's countenance, to trace the effect upon him of the refusal. How readily they follow the mood of the king! Vashti knows not what helping friends she has at court. Will they take sides with the weak against the strong? Ah, no! It will be more to their interest to pander to the weaknesses of the king. These smooth counsellors find it a very easy matter to persuade one who is already the slave to wine and wrath. Pretending to be afraid of the effect of Vashti's example upon their own spouses, they recommend that she shall be deposed from her position as Sultana, and another chosen in her place. They are astute enough not to suggest the putting away of one toy without having another to fill its place. They dilate so much on the offence of Vashti that Ahasuerus almost comes to think of himself as the most injured man in the world.

Was Vashti in the wrong? Some would say, Yes: wrong in that she yielded to petulance or pride, or to her sense of security in the affections of the king. It has been the constant practice to blame her; but there may be something to be said at least in extenuation of her conduct.

Let it be remembered how exclusive to this day are the customs of the East with respect to women. The same customs obtained in the time of Vashti. It was not the practice of Persian ladies to appear before any save their husbands, fathers, and sons. When women were found at the feast of Belshazzar, it was through the excesses to which wine and a lascivious idolatry had led. But the queen of Belshazzar was not present (Dan. v. 10), only women of lower rank and character. Hence, when Vashti refused, it was by reason of a custom which she knew the king would not have broken had he not been excited by wine.

Further, Vashti knew that the king, heated by his drinking, would expect that she and her maidens would please the multitude in a way not infrequent. He probably expected dances by the queen and maidens such as that by which, in after times, the daughter of Herodias pleased Herod.

The Jews have a tradition that the commands of the king were such as could not fail to shock a noble and high-spirited woman. But Vashti was possessed of a share of modesty and true queenliness very uncommon in those days ; and we strongly suspect that she was perfectly right in refusing to come at the king's command.

By the way in which the narrative is recorded, it would appear, at first sight, that Vashti was over-scrupulous and foolishly obstinate. It would seem as though she contumaciously objected to yield a trifling point. If, however, we knew more of the detail,—such as it did not appear necessary for the historian writing the Book of Esther, in the interest of the Jewish successor to Vashti and of the Jewish people, to insert,— we should probably not blame Vashti for obstinacy. If we may draw upon the knowledge which secular records of those times give, we shall be inclined rather to believe in the righteousness of Vashti's refusal.

But Vashti has been blamed, not only for disobeying the command of the king, but for refusing the request of her husband. Those who make this objection are those who hold that it is right for a wife to obey in every case her husband's will. She is to have no will but that of her husband. She is always to yield to the superior knowledge and power of the husband. One has put this idea in a quaint form, saying, that for a wife to act otherwise than in strict obedience, is "to set the rib above the head."

Now, where there is in reality superior intelligence on the part of the husband, it is sure to have sway. But this doctrine of implicit obedience on the part of the wife to one with whom she has contracted *mutual* obligations, is an absurdity as gross and heathenish as that into which Ahasuerus fell when he commanded Vashti to be exhibited before a crowd. His error was, in thinking that Vashti was simply his property —a slave queen, for whom his bare word was sufficient law. Many have fallen into the same error since. Marriage should be a state of mutual love, mutual help, and mutual concessions.

Paul exhorted women to obey their husbands; but he immediately added, "Husbands, love your wives, and be not bitter against them." He thus showed what sort of commands were to be obeyed. The law of love was to rule, and only such obedience as could be gained by love, required. A man is the head of the household, and in all questions relating thereto should have deference paid to his judgment. Especially should this be the case in questions concerning the external relationship of the family. But a wife is no more a slave than is an Englishman a slave to the monarch whom he acknowledges to be the head of the nation.

Husbands and wives are possessed of equal rights, such as may be claimed and allowed without detriment to the position of either. Ahasuerus did not recognize the rights of Vashti, but she was conscious of them. As a wife, she would do her duty, but not as a puppet or plaything. She thereby dared his power. She knew how terrible must be the consequences; but she was ready to meet the scorn that would be heaped upon her. All honour to one who in such times, in such a place, and under such circumstances, could dare to withstand the commands of her besotted lord. All honour to one who, taking her stand upon the inviolability and glory of her womanhood, could dare to do the right. Instead of blame for her obstinacy, let her have praise, as well for her moral courage as for her modesty.

It would be a good thing if many who are at this day drawn into scenes of pleasure and sensuous enjoyment would remember Vashti, and dare to do the right. Many women, upon whose faces a blush might shrink to find itself, might with advantage study the character, and strive to follow the example of Vashti. There is still need for the advice which an ancient orator gave to the daughters, sisters, and wives of his day—" to have their eyes painted with chastity, the words of God inserted in their ears, Christ's yoke tied to the neck, to be clothed with the silk of sanctity, the damask of devotion, and the purple of piety."

In Christian lands there is, we are glad to see, much true womanliness and modesty. It would be very painful to find any tendency to boldness and indelicacy among the wives and daughters of our day. It would be like taking all fragrance from the flowers and bloom from the peach. What is needed is, that there shall be withal a greater cultivation of all amiable and noble qualities, combined with a firm faith in the religion of the Saviour. This shall add a richer grace to all other graces. Without this faith, the one essential for a pure and perfect character is lacking. "There is beauty," says one, "in the blush of the rose, and there is a beauty of a higher character in the blush that mantles the cheek of modesty; but there may be as little loyalty to God in the animate as in the inanimate object." Faith in and love to God is most essential as the crown of womanly nature. We rejoice that in so many are found the qualities of amiability, modesty, and loyalty to God. All such will welcome Vashti as their sister.

It is something further to call forth praise, that modesty and moral courage were found

in one so *high in rank* as Vashti. Let it be
remembered that she was surrounded by many
things which would tend only to foster pride
and vanity. The influences of a life in a
harem must have been adverse to the development of all the finer and nobler qualities of
Vashti's nature. Yet she triumphed over them,
or she would not have risked rejection by her
husband and king, and refused to bend to that
which only a drunken humour suggested. Many
in less difficult circumstances would not have
been so firm and true. They would have ex-
cused the state of the king in the honour
conferred on themselves. Vanity would have
been flattered by being seated aloft, praised
and acknowledged as most beautiful, even
though by the side of a sottish king.

We can imagine the state of excitement
into which the women's court of Shushan
would be thrown when the inmates knew of
Vashti's refusal. The one who was accounted
their head, because most beautiful, to neglect
or withstand a command of the king their
master—unheard - of audacity ! Many would
doubtless deride her squeamishness. They
wished that it had only been their good fortune to receive such an invitation. And when
the determination of the king to cast her off
became known, doubtless many would rejoice,
and, tossing their heads, say, "The conceited
woman is rightly served." Such hoped, possibly
through her fall, to find a way to rise to his
majesty's favour.

Hard, indeed, she would find it, to bear the despite of her sister slaves. Overwhelming would seem the sudden rejection. How *unexpectedly* it came! That morning the sun of her prosperity rose bright in the heavens, but midday has not passed before her sky is darkened, and her sun has withdrawn itself. Henceforth she is left to wander in the courts of the women as the rejected queen.

We cannot but remark upon the facility with which divorce took place in that land of Persia. *How easily could the stronger cast off the weak!* Unjust and disastrous such a law. We cannot be too thankful that we live not where such laws obtain. Nor can we too jealously guard the sacred obligations of the wedded life. All must see with pain any increased carelessness about these obligations, and mark with sorrow the indications of domestic unhappiness revealed in divorce courts. Perhaps many cases of unhappiness might be traced to a similar cause to that which brought about the separation of Ahasuerus and Vashti. Any mere trifle becomes sufficient as an excuse for separation. We have heard of a quarrel and divorce taking place because one asserted that there were a certain number of windows in a house opposite, and the other denied it. Each maintained their point with obstinacy, and neglected to settle their difference by counting them. Indeed, such little things are the most fruitful cause of domestic unhappiness, leading on to the miserable exhibitions in public courts.

Many a poor sister of Vashti has, however, tasted Vashti's sorrow, owing to no fault in themselves. An indulgence in a like habit to that of Ahasuerus has led many to act with his foolishness, harshness, and injustice. Known only to themselves has been the dread of many a wife lest the knowledge of a husband's secret failing should get abroad. Known only to themselves the many shifts to make up for deficiencies for necessary household expenditure — deficiencies caused by a husband's extravagance and recklessness. Known only to themselves the number of weary hours during which they either sit watching or lie waking and waiting the return of their dissolute lord. Known only to themselves, also, the many insults, the ill-usage to which they are subject—ill-treatment, the result of inflamed passions and embittered spirits. God have mercy upon the thousands of sad women who know the truthfulness of that to which we refer! God have mercy, since men have so little!

The sneering utterance has sometimes been heard, that only women believe in Christianity. No wonder that the womanly heart turns to it for consolation, when there has been none found elsewhere. Far from thinking that it is a slight upon the Gospel, that more women believe it than men, we think it a high testimony to its value. Women have recognized the power of Christ and His Gospel. He has enfranchised them. We see what He has effected in this respect when we contrast lands under His sway with those that have not generally accepted the Gospel. How great the honour in which women are now held in these lands! Compare it with the tolerance accorded,—for toleration is all they get,—in unchristianized lands. We see, in the Vashtis of Persia, the zenanas of India, the houris of Turkey, and the squaws of the red man, what would have been the position of women in Europe, but for the principles which are the outgrowth of the Gospel.

Solomon, affecting to despise woman, said, "A man among a thousand have I found, but a woman among ten thousand I have not found." This was an utterance in harmony with the spirit of his age and nation. It would not be in harmony with the spirit of this age or of Christian nations. To this day the wife of the Jew occupies not a position equal to the wives of Christendom. Go into many synagogues and notice high barriers of brass in the galleries, behind which only women are allowed to sit, and through the bars of which they are permitted to catch glimpses of their fathers, husbands, or brothers, arrayed in the sacred fringed scarf, performing their devotions. In such a spot one realizes the breadth and boldness of the apostle's assertion, that "in Christ Jesus there is neither male nor female." Husbands and wives are in Him made "heirs together of the grace of life." In the Gospel they stand on a ground of perfect equality. The wife is only the "weaker vessel" in the same sense that the ornamental vase is more delicate, fragile, and tender than the homely and clumsy vessel which has been wrought from coarser clay.

How the Saviour honoured woman! What ready help He gave in all their troubles, and what unbounded confidence He received in return! It is most interesting to mark how He treated them. See the Canaanitish woman venturing to ask Him to come and restore her daughter, and He grants her request. See how the Samaritan woman at the well-side eagerly drinks in His utterances, and even forgets her errand in the absorbing character of His teachings. Behold Mary seated at His feet, forgetting her household cares, and how He forgives the forgetfulness. Notice Martha troubled about much serving, fretfully complaining of her burdens, and how He calms the fretfulness. Listen to His high encomium on another—"She hath done what she could." Hearken to the praise unstintingly given to the widow who, loving her temple and God more than herself, cast in "all the living that she had." Remember also how thoughtful was Christ for the one who stood in the nearest earthly relationship to Himself—His mother. He stayed for a time the full accomplishment of His work and of the world's redemption, to attend the sorrow of her through whose soul the sword of anguish was even then passing. Committing her into the hands of a loved disciple, He pronounced the words, " It is finished," and yielded His spirit into the hands of His Father.

Women also readily recognized His sympathy, and sought to repay in a measure His marked defence. They "ministered unto Him of their substance." They were among the last to leave the place of crucifixion, and the first to be at the tomb of His resurrection. The heart of woman has ever since been drawn to Christ. Had Vashti, the rejected queen, the divorced wife, the wronged woman, lived afterwards and known Him, she would, doubtless, have been among His followers. We detect in her that spirit which, although repudiating the commands of a Persian despot, would have recognized His holy claims. She lived up to the light she had ; and certainly all that was modest, pure, courageous, and womanly in her would be approved by Him. Divorced by man, we believe certainly that she was not disgraced before God.

CYRUS:

THE DIVINELY-DIRECTED DELIVERER.

Scripture Reference—II. *Chron.* xxxvi. 22.

OVE of country is a feeling deeply implanted in the heart. In none has it been more strongly planted than in the heart of the Jew of past ages. God had promised him the land, had given the land, and it was a delightsome land. It was a sort of Switzerland, with numerous natural defences, as well as productive powers. It had a metropolis, "the joy of the whole earth," a temple, "beautiful for situation" and favoured by the divine presence. After the Babylonian invasion however the land was desolated, and the temple desecrated. Strangers and aliens were scattered over the ruined nation. Wild beasts devoured it. Its vineyards were trampled, its olive gardens were burned, its fields were weed-covered, its terraces crumbled, its walls were broken down, and its glory had departed. Ichabod was written visibly on the face of the whole country. The Jew in captivity had hung his harp on the willow, and mingled

his tears with the waters of Babylon's river, as
he remembered Zion.

One generation passed away, that which had
seen the glory of Judæa, and another had
come. These only knew the past glory by hear-
say, but they kept it still in mind, and when
tempted to forget the days of their fathers in the
allurements of the land of their captivity, said,
"If I forget thee, O Jerusalem, let my right
hand forget her cunning." Many hoped to return, but their prospects were of the dreariest
description, their hopes at the lowest ebb. They
hardly dared to breathe their hopes, and to acknowledge that they were Jews. There were
prophecies as to their return, but where was the
man who should be instrumental in their fulfilment? It seemed absurd to cherish the hope. The
dark night seemed endless, and no star pierced
the black pall. But God's own good time of
brightening came; came most unexpectedly and
suddenly, for God stirred up the spirit of Cyrus,
king of Persia.

God stirred up Cyrus to do a *great and necessary work*. If prophecy was to be fulfilled, the
land to be reclaimed, the temple rebuilt, the
people saved from extermination, the divine
worship restored, national prosperity introduced,
the way prepared for the advent of Him who
was to be the Saviour of the world, some one
must act. Cyrus is specially incited to the
work. That work may not have seemed half so
glorious as some other work he performed. But

promoting the arts of peace is much better than all the glamour and glory of war, building up is far nobler than breaking down and destroying good. Many at this day think far more of business, politics, art and science, as being of the highest importance to the welfare of men, but nothing is so truly important as to spread religion and build up men in faith. In this the most obscure Christian can engage.

Cyrus was a *fitting instrument* for the great work. He is said to have been a man of such noble character that some have thought he had no actual existence, but was only a myth, a creature of the brain. Herodotus said that "he ruled his subjects like a father." Xenophon calls him "the model prince." Plutarch asserts that "in wisdom and greatness of soul he excelled all other kings." Ezra bears testimony (ch. i. 2, 3) to his piety, deep feeling, and self-sacrifice. He was a fitting instrument to carry out the divine purposes. God can work through any instrumentality, but there is always a fitness in the man selected for any great work. As a dull tool is not chosen by the skilled artificer, when a sharp one is at hand, so God does not choose unsuitable men for any agency. As in nature things are adapted to the purpose they are to serve, so in grace. Those chosen are not always those whom men would select; but God knows best, for He sees the heart. He makes the sheep-boy a king, and,—in modern history,—a farmer may become a statesman, and a rail-splitter or a canal boatman a President. They are not the men who would have been selected as the most probable leaders of men, but God in his providence raiseth up one and putteth down another. The hearts of kings are as "rivulets of water" in His hand. He turneth them whithersoever He will. Hence He stirred up Cyrus, pagan though he was, to do a great and necessary work and to be the deliverer of His people from captivity.

God has various means whereby to incite to action. Among those things which may have stirred up Cyrus may have been the teaching, pleading or influence of Daniel, or the record of God's dealing with Nebuchadnezzar. It may have been that the very success that had been granted to him aroused in him real gratitude. Or it is possible that he knew of the prophecies uttered by Isaiah concerning himself, and especially that one so personal, "I girded thee though thou hast not known Me, etc." (Isaiah xlv. 5). He is spoken of as "Cyrus, the anointed of the Lord," before whom the "two leaved gates of brass" were to be opened. And the gates of Babylon, answering to that description, were opened before him.

On his heart, too,—as on the heart of an Abimelech or an Ahasuerus,—God acted by His holy Spirit, stirring him up to the necessary work.

The Divine incitement to the necessary work was at a *most opportune time.* It was at the end of the seventy years that had been foretold by the prophet as the period of the captivity. The land had had her Sabbaths of rest. Awful indeed had been "the grey and silent Sabbaths that had fallen on Judah's cities and fields." Now the time of Babylon's judgment and Judah's release is to come ; " And it shall come to pass when seventy years are accomplished that I will punish the king of Babylon, etc." (Jer. xxv. 12).

Daniel and many pious Jews were doubtless at this time praying for the accomplishment of the promise, but they could not see how the prophecy was to be fulfilled. When the appointed time, however, is come, God's agent appears. As it was at midnight that God visited the Egyptians and delivered Israel, so it was at midnight that he visited the Babylonians and opened a way of escape for Judah. At midnight in Belshazzar's palace carousings profane and obscene took place, and then was seen the mystic handwriting of Divine judgment on the wall. While the king gazes in horror, the cry is heard, " The enemy comes !" Cyrus and his army having succeeded in their plan of diverting the waters of the Euphrates were at that moment marching by the drained bed of the river into the very heart of the city. " On that night was Belshazzar the king of the Chaldeans slain ;" the Babylonian power was supplanted by the Persian, and the fitting instrument for accomplishing the restoration of the Jews was known to have appeared at the right moment.

God teaches His instruments *how* as well as *when* to act. Cyrus was "stirred up" to seek to include others in the work. He issued his proclamation and stimulated others, who desired to return, to act. He had it in his heart to rebuild the temple, but of what avail the temple without worshippers? Hence he sought to arouse others to effort, to self-sacrifice, to readiness, to dedicate of their substance to God. He gave liberally, returning that which Nebuchadnezzar had taken from the temple, and which he might have retained as booty. In addition to the vessels of gold which Nebuchadnezzar had taken from Jerusalem, he gave thirty chargers of gold and a thousand chargers of silver (Ezra i. 7-11). The number of the vessels altogether were five thousand four hundred. Such liberality amazed the people. They could hardly believe their eyes and ears. They were as "those that dreamed." Their mouths were "filled with laughter." They burst out in song, saying, "The Lord hath done great things for us, whereof we are glad." Great was the influence of the action of Cyrus. Oh what great results follow the Divine stirrings of heart in those who have position or wealth, or even in those who are obscure.

We should recognize the Divine stirrings in individual souls. If a work presents itself, enter on it. If an impulse to act generously should come, act upon it. If a conviction should force itself upon us that certain habits should be broken, follow it. Recognize, too, the Divine stirrings in the movements of our times. We have no need to be restless, for God knows what will come, and always raises up men to accomplish his work. With respect to the Church there is much over which we have to mourn—variance between sects, worldliness, latitudinarianism, and unbelief—but we believe that God is stirring in men's hearts, and that a brighter day is about to dawn.

As the Lord stirred the spirit of Cyrus, so He *can stir men now*. Cyrus under the Divine incitement seemed to lay hold of a bell rope and to tug vehemently to toll the death knell of a cruel, idolatrous, tyrannous system. As he tolled, the mighty fabric of Babylonish pride toppled and fell, and great was the fall of it. The echo of that tolling is heard still adown the centuries, telling us that as Belshazzar's power fell, so, sooner or later, all that is false, despotic, oppressive, unrighteous, shall vanish; and just as Cyrus tolled the destruction of Babylon one hour, and sent out the next hour his pealing proclamation that the house of the Lord should be built, so now let the peal of praise be heard that God's work is making progress, that truth, justice, peace, liberty and righteousness shall triumph, and triumph everlastingly. Oh, how we rejoice in all the success of Christ's cross up to the present, and long for the time to come when every heart shall adore Him, love Him, every knee bow to Him, and every tongue confess that He is Lord, to the glory of God the Father.

THE DEVOUT DAMASCENE; OR
ANSWERED WHILE ASKING.

SCRIPTURE REFERENCE—*Gen.* xv. 2, xxiv. 1-67.

HEN Abraham came into Syria by way of Damascus, he probably found this Eliezer, who became not only a sort of bailiff but a trusted friend. He had been selected by Abraham to be his heir, but of course when Isaac was born, he could not hold that position. He became honoured as "the eldest servant of his (Abraham's) house, that ruled over all that he had" (Gen. xxiv. 2). To him probably was committed the delicate business recorded in this chapter; and the way in which it was executed was just that which would be expected from one who had so won the confidence of Abraham as to be selected as his heir.

We cannot but admire the thoughtfulness of Abraham for his son. He sought to prevent Isaac from being brought under the polluting influence of the Canaanitish people in the midst of whom he dwelt. He also desired to prevent Isaac from going back to the country from which he had himself been divinely led. Hence he sends his steward to select, from among his kindred, one who shall be a suitable life companion for his son. He takes an oath of his steward that he will in no wise permit a wife to be taken for his son among the Canaanites, or lead Isaac to Mesopotamia again.

The mission of Eliezer was indeed difficult and delicate. We must not think of it according to the customs of our land. In oriental nations, to this day, it is the practice to employ a third person to negotiate a marriage between those who seem by report to be suitable for such relationship. Eliezer undertook the affair with every desire to gratify his master, and to serve well even the one who had supplanted him in heirship. We cannot too highly praise " the man " for his unselfishness, or too warmly admire the devoutness which characterized his whole conduct. He sought by prayer success from God. The prayer recorded here was probably not the first he had offered with respect to the subject. His mission was not only delicate, but rather indefinite. He is sent to the relations of his master to choose from among them a wife for Isaac. He knows that much of the satisfaction of Abraham and of the welfare of Isaac will depend on his right performance of his duty. He feels the responsibility resting upon him, and makes every needful preparation for discharging it. He starts on the camels prepared, and carries with him suitable presents. After a long journey he arrives at a city in Mesopotamia, where dwells Nahor, his master's brother. It is eventide when he reaches the well outside the city. The graceful daughters of the city, with pitchers poised on their shoulders, are just coming forth to draw water for their households. The camels turn their long necks and weary eyes in the direction of the approaching maidens. They know that on their arrival the dry troughs, which till now have only tantalized their thirst, will be filled. The shade from the palm trees avails not now to break the fierce rays of the sun, setting so rapidly in the west. Long shadows are over the landscape. Eliezer stands with the golden light about him. He feels that this may be the critical moment. Clasping firmly his hands, and lifting fervently his face heavenwards, he breathes the beautiful prayer, "O Lord God of my master Abraham, I pray thee, send me good speed this day and shew kindness unto my master Abraham." It was a brief prayer, because there was not time to say much more; but it was appropriate. He asked for what he felt he needed. He did not use prayer as a mere mystical method of pleasing God, but as the expression of a felt need. This is true prayer. God does not want fine words, long sentences, or wearying repetitions. None are heard for their "much speaking." That is a heathenish notion. God is not glorified by the length of time we remain on our knees, or the number of words we are able to crowd into a certain time.

The longest prayers are often the most unmeaning. This is true of prayers in the home and in the church. Brief, earnest, sincere prayer is that which wings its way to heaven. When Peter was sinking in the waters his cry was brief and pointed enough, " Lord, save! I perish."

These remarks are not unnecessary, for so many will, even in respect to prayer, measure themselves by others. Many shrink from praying in public because they think that a longer supplication is expected than they feel they are able to offer. A brief utterance even expressing the desire to be in the spirit of prayer would often be far more acceptable to God and to man than the laboured and lengthy utterances which, if they have at first induced a praying spirit, have often afterwards banished it. Heart prayers are those God accepts ; but unmeant, made-up, formal prayers " He cannot away with." Newton says, " Many men pray not as expressing the desires of their fellows towards God, but as expressing God's commands to them."

Eliezer did not hesitate to ask God's guidance in respect to a subject which many would account as quite within the scope of their own judgment to decide. Many also would have thought it beneath the notice of God. Many would have made their way direct into the city to Nahor's house to choose for them-

selves. And many would have left the matter
to be decided by chance; but Eliezer seeks guidance from God. Only those who are ignorant
of the value of trifles, of their relative power, or
who are ignorant of the fact that there are no
trifles but which may become all-important
circumstances, would think such an affair
as that Eliezer had in hand, as beneath God's
notice ; and if not beneath God's notice, it may
properly be the subject of prayer. Many who
contemplate forming relationships might with
the greatest advantage imitate the example of
Eliezer in this case, and seek direction from
God. Were this the practice there would be fewer
unhappy marriages. Eliezer in carrying out his
master's wish seeks success from God.

At the *most suitable time* the steward
prays. He committed his way unto the Lord
at the period when he felt most strongly that he
needed His guidance. God honours the man's
trust. "It came to pass that *before he had done
speaking* Rebekah came out." She was the
very one whom God had appointed. She knew
not that she was moving to fulfil the intention
of God. In her acts and in her words she was
doing that which was in harmony with the sign
the man had asked. Courteously, on being
asked for a draught from her vessel, she offered
even to draw for the camels also. In the very
first person he addressed Eliezer had the answer
to his prayer. Thus in Isaiah (lxv. 24) it is said,
" Before they call I will answer, etc.," and in

Daniel (ix. 23), "At the *beginning* of thy supplications the commandment came forth."

Some have doubts about the power of prayer, but God disturbs not His laws by answering prayer; He has doubtless so arranged law that prayer can be answered in harmony with a higher law. It would at one time have seemed impossible that men should hear one another's voices when many many miles away from each other, but science has shewn this and even more wondrous things to be quite possible. We shall come one day to believe that which the true believer has verified by experience, that God does answer prayer. We lose much of the comfort of prayer because, after we have put up a petition, we rather forget to look for the answer, or because we have but a semi-belief in the power of prayer. If a prayer be a reality to us it is no less so in God's sight. Some put up prayer in the spirit which seems to say, "Now I will see whether God will answer that or not." God is not to be subjected to mere testings. Christ showed that when on earth He refused to gratify the curiosity of the Pharisees or submit to the tests they had prepared for Him. Where God is perfectly trusted, the answer will in some way or other overtake or even anticipate the prayer.

The rapidity of the answer to the man's prayer completely astonished him. "He, wondering at her, held his peace," waiting to know whether the "Lord had made his journey prosperous or not." God not only answered speedily, but in the exact manner desired. Sometimes He sends the answer in a way so different from that we expected, that we discern not the fact that we have an answer. But what heavenly telegraphy is here ! No sooner is the petition sent than the answer is given. The very correspondence between the sign desired and its rapid fulfilment only sets Eliezer speculating as to whether it may have been nothing more than a remarkable coincidence rather than a Divine response. Meanwhile he acts as though he believed. He offers to Rebekah the gifts which indicated already his business. He offers such as shall become the character of his master, who was princely in his possessions as well as position. He offers and waits. The man " held his peace." He knows that if God has answered in part He will also answer fully. God's dealings should always induce awe and patient waiting. He will often surprise us with the blessings of goodness. In our own lives we have probably known similar cases of surprisingly rapid answers to prayer, so rapid, perhaps, that we have even disbelieved in the answer. What if God had withdrawn the help or blessing given, because received in such unbelief ! There are times when we, like Eliezer, and like the Israelites on the shores of the Red Sea, have to be still and know that the Lord is God. Then God's action staggers belief.

Eliezer enquires of the maiden whether there

is room in her father's house for him to lodge. After the manner of the orientals she readily replies, " We have both straw and provender enough and room to lodge in." He follows Rebekah. Laban acts as host in place of his father Bethuel. He welcomes Eliezer heartily. " Come in, thou blessed of the Lord, etc." Eliezer enters and attends to the wants of his men and camels, but will not attend to his own until he has unburdened his mind. He tells of his errand and of the meeting with Rebekah at the well, of his praying, of the speedy answer, and of the sign fulfilled. Laban and Bethuel are surprised, and see in it God's hand. They say, " The thing proceedeth from the Lord, we cannot speak unto thee good or ill." Then the man " bowed his head and worshipped." Rebekah consented to accompany him, and became the wife of Isaac, his master's son. Everything fell out better than the steward could have expected; he could only see in it God's hand, God's mercy in guiding him and in confirming his hope.

God is as willing to answer us as to answer Eliezer of Damascus. Prayer can overcome difficulties that seem insurmountable. When the cup of sorrow is not removed, the strength is given to bear it, and so prayer is answered. If the way we expected does not open up in answer to our supplication, another and better is sure to be made plain. Prayer also " makes the darkened cloud withdraw."

When in the clearer light of another world we look back at our past life, we shall all see that God has answered all prayers that it would have been for our good to have answered, and that in others the withholdment has been the kindliest response. Then we shall "bow our heads and worship" Him who made our earthly journey prosperous, and who has brought us to the "city which hath foundations." Whatever, then, our anxiety—trial—perplexity, let us lay all before God. If we are earnestly longing for the salvation of members of our own family, or for the advancement of God's kingdom, let us by prayer and supplication make our requests known unto God; and He will send us an answer of peace, even as He did to Eliezer.

REBEKAH; OR THE WORTH OF LIFE.

SCRIPTURE REFERENCE—*Genesis* xxvii. 46.

THIS was the question of one who had planned certain methods of securing great joy, but who found her plans frustrated. Rebekah schemed and sinned for Jacob, but he had to flee away from home on account of those schemings and so she lost him. The other son, Esau, was estranged from her and would follow his own wayward bent. Thus, disappointed in both, Rebekah in her bitterness exclaims, " What good shall my life do me ! "

Some have been asking in very shrill tones, the question, " Is life worth living ? " Such a question is a reflection on the beneficence of Him who gave us life. It is the question moreover of those who have doubtless experienced great disappointments, or who have altogether failed in life.

God has given life for some definite purpose. We are to seek to know that purpose, and to strive to accomplish it. Circumstances, temperament, tastes, faculties, and desires may together indicate that special purpose. There is a position for each one to take in life, a niche for each to fill. To take that position, to fill well that suitable niche is to succeed.

The success for which men strive is varied according to occupation, position, training or powers. To the tradesman, a large shop in the leading thoroughfare of a great town or city, a numerous staff of assistants, and a long list of customers, is the ideal success. To the merchant it shapes itself in ample means, good credit, costly warehouses, extensive operations, a well furnished mansion in a suburb, and the respectful notice of those in higher rank. The artist dreams of pictures in the academy, on the line, with admiring crowds around them ;—the physician, of an extensive and aristocratic practice, and large consultation fees ;—the lawyer, of large estates to control and remunerative conveyances, or mortgage deeds to make out ;—the barrister, of important briefs and heavy retaining fees;— the scientist, of some secret he is to wring from nature, startling the world with its novelty ;— the explorer, of unknown tracts explored, and stirring accounts of adventure published ;—the warrior, of being praised by his chiefs and gazetted for loftiest honour ;—the politician, of wide influence, party power and plenteous patronage ;—and the preacher, of rich livings and great congregations. Now these are all worldly ideas of success. Many have much

loftier ideals.   An artist can care more for
truthfulness in art than for his own pecuniary
advancement.   A politician may care more for
his country's honour, for the triumph of justice
and liberty in his own and other lands, and for
the elevation and well-being of the masses of
his fellows, than for all personal advancement,
party power or royal favour.   A preacher also,
may esteem far above large salaries, social pres-
tige and crowded congregations, the joy of
seeing souls brought to Christ, or he may desire
to see the acknowledgment of some long overlooked truth, the triumph of pure principles, the
increase of the truest charity, and the fall of all
unnecessary bigoted and prejudicial divisions.
These are higher types of success.   To help
forward any of these ideas is to succeed in a
measure, to see them fully triumph is satisfactory success.

Failure is a dreary Sahara where all hopefulness is in danger of being burnt up.   Or, we
may compare it to the Arctic regions where the
life blood is frozen and effort crushed.   Success
is the stimulating sunny temperate or tropical
region where joy is supposed to flourish as the
palm tree.   The latter is certainly the more
attractive region as a dwelling place.   Nor is it
wrong to desire to dwell there if we can do so
without sacrifice of principle.   Some imagine
that if we have success and joy in this life we
must necessarily lose it in the next.   We cannot
however, admit that failure here is the best

preparation even for joys hereafter. There is no niggardliness in the Divine arrangements, preventing any from getting anything beyond a certain amount of joy out of existence here or hereafter. It is quite possible to gain success in this life without losing it in the next, for religion has " the promise of the life that now is, and of that which is to come."

There is *failure which is success, and success which is a failure.* When prophets and apostles, and heralds of the cross were rejected and perhaps martyred, the world might say, " what failures are the efforts and the lives of such men ! " Subsequent ages reverse the verdict. When a temporary success is gained by questionable and unlawful means, such success, however gilded and praised, is in reality failure.

Some, however, care not about means, they only want to be shown a plain, rapid, and sure way to worldly success. They want to find the royal road to wealth. Many are ready to do anything if only thereby they may gain largely and mount to the height of their ambition. They will sacrifice conscience or securely gag it. Such will borrow and have no intention of repaying the amount, they will incur debts they never contemplate discharging; they will arrange accounts so that the poorest account can be gathered of their affairs ; will suddenly " break" in order to "make" themselves. They succeed in one sense, but what a poor success, and what a price they pay for it ! So in higher than business realms, there is a meretricious, glittering, showy success gained by shuffle and scheming, by cleverness, chicanery and cunning, by double-dealing and indifference to all principles of truth and justice, but it is as demoralizing as it is detestable, as ruinous as it is iniquitous. Let us make no mistake about the nature of the success at which we aim. Let it be true, beneficial, worthy, permanent, and such as we can venture to submit to the Divine for approval.

Now there are *certain recognized principles of success* in worldly things, and these principles apply in the building up of character. Success has to be gained. It is not waiting, like some obsequious servant, to pour its treasures into our hands. Personal and persistent effort has to be put forth to win it. Effort will generally bring it. Discouragements and difficulties may be great, but they can be overcome and the object gained. The men of mark in the great cotton district, are men who were persistent, and were determined to succeed. They learned the secrets of their business in its every stage, and,—as it is said in Manchester,—"began life in their shirt sleeves." By depending on themselves, and not on what parents or relatives had done before them, by thrift and toil they rose.

One of the worst illusions of life is to be constantly waiting for good fortune to come to us, by the death of some rich relative, or by meeting with some one who shall recognize our superlative talents. Effort and toil injure us not, if only we cultivate habits of temperance, and of probity. Only that success which is the result of effort is that which is greatly to be desired.

Amongst other conditions of advance are the *avoidance of certain indulgences, carefulness about trifles, and attention to details.* The little leakages, if unattended to, sink the ship. The minute must be looked after as well as the massive. Every inch gained in the struggle must be held. Every step climbed should make the ascent the easier. Neglect of trifles may damage far beyond conception, but attended to, their power for helping our advance accumulates. To be unpunctual; giving greater care to the adornment of the body than of the mind; indulging in late rising, or in excessive eating or drinking; to be constantly dependent on the narcotic weed or on stimulants for energy; to risk small amounts as stakes in various games; to spend the sabbaths in novel reading, and every evening in the mere search for amusement will never bring success. Moreover to neglect the cultivation of courteous and gentle manners, to pretend to be a rough diamond because you don't like the pain of the polishing wheel, will also militate against success. To get into debt beyond what we have reasonable assets wherewith to pay, is sure to check success. The mind hampered by the thought of debt cannot be well balanced and clear. Rash schemes are likely to be devised, and speculations entered upon which may bring ruin. That which leads to much debt is the acquiring of lofty ideas as to the scale of personal and domestic expenditure. So many wish to be measured by the house they live in, or by the furniture with which it is garnished, rather than by their own characters or brains, or purpose in life.

Again, to neglect honestly to see, at regular intervals, what is our position, is a sure way of missing success. Some are above attention to figures. They spend the pounds and neglect the pennies. They go on, perhaps, for months and years, ignorant of how much their expenditure has exceeded their income ; they make drafts on the principal time after time, until, at length, they find a draft dishonoured and themselves beggared. An honest balancing of books at certain periods, curtailment of unnecessary personal, domestic, and even business expenditures would save many from failure and lead to solid success.

Now these are matters with which all are familiar enough, but they are well-worn ruts in which it is safe to move. Your own minds assent to their truth.

There are sometimes chances which militate against success in some particular direction ; a man may have a bad start, or unsuitable training, or he may have taken a false step which has hampered him all through life, and will cause him to stagger along to the end. On the other hand there are favourable circumstances or unexpected associations which may materially help towards success. The favourable circumstances sometimes appear to be the result of chance. Men speak of their "good fortune." Certain men seem to get into the very current which sweeps on directly to success. Everything they touch seems to prosper. We must not, however, think that such events and lives are only the result of chance. There is a "Providence which shapes" the life and end of every man. "Promotion cometh neither from the east, nor from the west, nor from the south; but God is the judge, He putteth down one and raiseth up another." "God was with Joseph and he was a prosperous man." Often by our wilfulness we frustrate the good designs of God towards us. He has even at times to permit our plans to be thwarted and hopes blighted, that we may learn our dependence on Him. When we succeed we should not think of it as chance, but as an evidence of God's mercy, and God's will must be taken into account in all our plans for success.

Another condition of success is *to be able to wait*, to exercise patience. This is a God-like quality. By waiting and holding our own, we often see the right opportunity come to us. Anyhow, even if we fail we should still be persistent in any good object, learning from past failures to compel future successes.

That success which comes too early is not always the best. It may make us over-confident.

We may set our minds on something which, if it came, would be our greatest hindrance. Abraham Lincoln, when seeking to get into Congress, was once beaten. Informed of his defeat, he did not spend breath in vain regrets, nor in upbraiding others. In the felt inward strength of purpose he uttered words which after years endorsed : " This defeat will make me President!" But for that defeat Lincoln might never have put forth the mighty energy which showed him to be the foremost man in the Republic, and which made him the champion and deliverer of the millions of an oppressed race. Over-confidence is equivalent to failure. An army easily gaining a victory, gives up carefulness and may yield to indulgences which will afterwards make it a prey and a spoil. The conquered and despised may rise against them with lion-like courage, and struggle intensely until victory forsakes the banners of the over-confident, and rests on those of the once defeated. Early success must be followed up with vigour or it may only allure to failure.

It would be well if men would *moderate their ideas of success.* Some will not be content unless they attain to the greatest wealth and loftiest position. There is a feverishness in men leading to exhaustive effort. Especially is this the case in the pursuit of wealth. Even when many have sufficient of this world's goods they eagerly desire more. Expanding desires chain men to the wheel of business until they sink, bruised and broken, to die.

Further, if a man in the struggle to acquire wealth has *neglected every opportunity of improving his mind, or tastes,*—if he has lost his cheerfulness or hopefulness, or his health, what shall balance the loss? If to gain position he has sacrificed self-respect, if to rise in society he has sunk in sincerity, again we ask what shall balance the loss?

We believe that many who never attain to the position of being accounted wealthy, or seeing their names prominent in daily papers, have yet gained a true success in that they are pure, sincere, gentle, charitable and devout in spirit. Such qualities are better than a large balance at the bankers, or the applause of a thoughtless multitude. Business is a fine school for the development of some of the noblest qualities in man. There are men in business now who occupy in the esteem of the circle in which they move, a position such as many a statesman and even monarch might envy.

In thinking of how to succeed in life, Wolsey's words to Cromwell are well worthy of being remembered. He charged him to

"Fling away ambition.
By that sin fell the angels; how can man then,
The image of his Maker, hope to win by it?
Love thyself last: cherish those hearts that hate thee,
Corruption wins not more than honesty;
Still in thy right hand carry gentle peace
To silence envious tongues. Be just and fear not."

It cannot always be said that " honesty is the best policy." Sometimes justice and dishonesty have a temporary outward success. If, however, we take into account the approval of conscience, and look not to the present but to the future, we shall see that honesty *is* the best policy. We must look to that future, and remember that only that life, which God will pronounce good, has been really a success. If we spoil life here it will affect our life in the next world, just as the gash on one side of the page of a book cuts the narrative on the opposite side. We want to reach that other world and gain approval there as well as here. Our success here should not be such as to shame us there. The roots of the water lily strike downwards into the mud of the lake, yet it sends up a long stem which bears on the surface of the water leaves of beauty and flowers of fragrance. So should our lives send on to the other world such results, that our God may look upon them with approval.

Success should mean satisfaction. Many, however, attain worldly success but have no real satisfaction in their souls. They say at the end of life in the bitterness of their spirits " What good shall my life do me ? " They are amazed with the poverty of past results, great as these may seem to their fellows. There is a craving for something undefined. What is the meaning of the dissatisfaction and craving? This, that earthly success can never fully satisfy a spirit fitted to be filled by God's love. The common experience is that the world cannot satisfy. Why do men try the experiment so long? Only God in Christ can give true satisfaction and peace to our spirits. We must see our sinfulness, our lack of that which can form a claim for mercy, our failures, and our spiritual helplessness ere we can find peace with Christ. To have succeeded by honesty, justice and truth only after the fashion of the world, and to have come to the end of life without having Christ as the Saviour is as unwise as it would be for an engineer to throw a number of arches over a broad river, and to leave the last arch unbuilt. The last being unbuilt, the whole would be useless for the heavy vehicle or swiftly-flying express. How many leave the last spiritual arch unbuilt! All have to cross, sometime and somehow, the river of death, or be swept away by it. Crowds like an advancing army press on behind and there is no going back. "What shall we do in the swellings of Jordan?" And "what shall it profit a man if he gain the whole world and lose his own soul?" Oh let us seek Christ, and count all things but loss for the excellency of the knowledge of Christ Jesus our Lord. We must trust in Him who was content to be accounted as failing in life, that He might succeed in atoning for our sins. He gave Himself up for us, and when He now looks upon a soul, penitently turning to His Cross, "He sees of the travail of His soul and is satisfied."

Rebekah fixed her mind on one thing that should give her real satisfaction; should make her life of worth to her; should, in fact, make it a success, but she had to bear with disappointment. She schemed, but succeeded not. Life seemed not of such great worth to her. And it must be always so, unless we seek satisfaction in God, and leave ourselves, our families, and our undertakings, in His hands.

Whatever then may be our lot, let us seek that godliness which is great gain. Better far to have adversity in this world than loss in the next. If we have prosperity, let us take it as from God, and use it for His glory; if adversity, let us bear it in His strength. Let there be no pride in prosperity or murmuring in adversity. Pray that if riches increase the heart may not be set upon them, and that if worldly success be denied the heavenly may not be missed.

HOBAB: OR POSSIBLE USEFULNESS.

SCRIPTURE REFERENCE— *Numbers* x. 29—32.

IT has been supposed that Hobab was only another name for Job, and there is similarity in the name. This is most uncertain. There has been great difficulty in ascertaining who he was, and as to whether he was identical with Jethro,—spoken of in *Exodus* xviii. 2.

The word translated "father-in-law" also means "relation," and Hobab may have been a relative or brother accompanying Jethro. Anyhow he came to Moses at Sinai. He finds that the one whom he had known as a shepherd has now become the leader of a great nation. Circumstances have changed. Moses is not, however, ashamed of those with whom he was formerly associated. Miriam and Aaron appear to have despised Zipporah (*Num.* xii. 1), but Moses welcomed Hobab, and even besought him to remain with them.

Two years have probably passed over since the deliverance from Egypt. The Hebrew civil

and ecclesiastical system is now in order. The
Israelites are journeying steadily onward when
Hobab meets with them. Acquainted with the
desert, he might be of great service to them,
and Moses invites and persuades him to cast in
his lot with Israel.

Moses uses several arguments. He suggested that the Israelites *had a bright prospect.* And the Christian has the same. He
knows that "life and immortality have been
brought to light."

The Israelites also had a *sure promise.* "The
Lord hath spoken good concerning Israel."
Moses himself had faith in that promise. God's
promise is something satisfactory to rest upon.
A revelation is something far more reliable than
mere instincts and desires. We don't want
mere uncertainties or guesses, but a "sure word
of prophecy."

Moses urged as the strongest argument the
service Hobab might render. He might be to
them as "eyes." He would have knowledge
of wells, of the tracks of the dangerous tribes
and districts. To help others is a greater
satisfaction than to be helped. This argument
therefore would weigh strongly with Hobab.
And this idea should weigh with those who
look on Christianity without giving definite adhesion to it. It should not be a question in respect to religion as to what we can gain, but
what we can give; not what strength we shall obtain, but what cheer we can contribute to others

Moses further expressed to Hobab the *readiness*, on the part of himself and the Israelites to *confer benefit on him.* " We will do thee good." Of some society it cannot be said that to be mixed up in it is beneficial, but in true Christian society there is always found that which brightens and encourages those struggling against life's temptations, difficulties, discouragements, and disappointments.

There was also a readiness on the part of Moses to *share with* Hobab any of the *unexpected* blessings the Lord might bestow. " Whatever good the Lord should show" was to be participated in. There is always greater joy to be experienced than anything we have yet known in our Christian life. We cannot exhaust the power of our God. His bestowals are not measured by our deserts but by His own love. He is ever beforehand with us in His readiness to bless, and divine surprises are ever in store for those who love God.

Pathetic was the appeal of Moses, " Leave us not we pray thee." It has the same tone of intensity that is found in that utterance of Paul, " I beseech you by the mercies of God that ye present your bodies a living sacrifice;" or of that of Christ, " Come unto me all ye that labour and are heavy laden, and I will give you rest." Christians should be ready constantly to repeat the invitation. Ministers also should repeat the invitation with emphasis;—not with command, but with affection. Indirect as well as direct influence should be used to induce others to come. Tales with a moral too pointed become painful. The moral must be wrapped up, hidden. So invitations to come to Christ should not be put so pointedly as to repel. Formal preaching or professional evangelism is likely to produce hypocrites, not true Christians. Anything approaching cold artificiality is most damaging. Gentle, indirect, loving influence produces the greatest effect. The sun does not say to the seed, "Now I am about to make you spring up, you shall grow, whether you will or not;" but the sun begins by shining and by sending down its bright rays to warm, expand, fructify the seed, and bring the tender blade to the surface. Thus in all endeavours to spread Christ's truth and win others to Him, love and true sympathy will have far more effect than all formal, artificial, dogmatic utterances. Threats may effect at times what love cannot perform, but few after all will be driven to accept religion !

Many are strangers to the love of God because of the way in which He has been misrepresented. Suppose a father going on service to India should leave a young child to the care of a nurse, who, always speaking of her master as strict, firm, commanding, gives gradually an impression to the child that is very different from that which should be given. The child is constantly told, if you don't do this and that, your father will not love you. At last tidings are brought that the father is coming back.

The child looks forward with fear. When the father comes in, the child is shy, trembling, troubled. The father is perplexed. His child fears to come to him. He asks, What means this fear and hesitancy? The child replies, " I feared you would never receive or care for me, because I knew I have not perfectly kept all you wrote down in the book you left behind. I feared you would not love me if I were not perfect." How the joy of the parent in his return would be clouded by the pain at finding how wrongly he had been represented to his dear child during his absence. And our heavenly Father has ofttimes to bear with such misrepresentations on the part of those who should make him known in His merciful, loving character.

The *result* of the invitation and pleading in Hobab's case is a little uncertain. At first he declined but probably consented subsequently. We find afterwards that his descendants reaped advantage from association with Israel (cf. Judges i. 16. I. Sam. xv. 6). The Kenites were spared because of kindness shewn to Israel, but when they came into full relationship they came in on less advantageous grounds. There is always loss also occasioned by delay in matters of religion. When any question of spiritual importance is before us, there should be no hesitancy, but a clear-minded, firm, devout decision, especially remembering how great service we may render to others.

SCRIPTURE REFERENCE—*John* iv. 14.

INTEREST may be found in gazing at some fountain standing in the street or by a roadside, rude in construction, or ornate in carving, with a group of russet-clad or quaintly - attired women around, waiting to fill the jars they so deftly carry on their heads or poise on their shoulders. Many have depicted such a scene to the delight of others. But around no fountain ever gathered more of interest than around that mentioned in this chapter.

The wearied Jesus lingers outside a Samaritan city while His disciples enter to buy food. A low stone wall, surrounding a well, offers a welcome resting place. A woman of Samaria, in the blue, ungirded attire of her race, comes to the well and silently draws water. As she places the narrow-necked jar on her head, and is about to move homewards, she is detained by a request from the Saviour. At first she had felt some antipathy to the stranger as she furtively noticed that He was a Jew; but after some conversation with Him, she looked upon Him with awe, not only because He claimed to be greater than Jacob, but to be the actual Messiah, and to have the power of giving the water which would "spring up into everlasting life."

Now we are concerned in this assertion of the divine Saviour, therefore, let us note *how unique is the character of that which Christ professes to be able to bestow.* Christ's truth, Christ's life, Christ's work, Christ's personal and living sympathy, are the waters of life. The knowledge of them gives life spiritual and eternal. Nothing can give spiritual life but the truth of Christ. Man has the ordinary animal life, can enjoy social life, and find absorption in business and pleasure, but these are not the whole of life. Man's soul has needs which the world cannot satisfy. Man must know of the mercy and love of God. He needs to know that his sins can be pardoned, and that he can be received fully into the favour of God. Where can he find this knowledge? Neither nature nor philosophy can assure him of this. If he should find much that indicates the beneficence of the Creator, he also must find evidences of sternness which shake his faith. The sufferings inflicted by parasites, by beasts of prey, earthquakes, storms, diseases, and disasters, speak of a terrible power in which little mercy can be traced. A soul under spiritual anxiety can gain little consolation from the contemplation of nature. And what can it gain as it comes in view of the dark mystery of death? At such a time the soul longs after certain assurance from one who has authority to give it. It longs for light, for love, which is life. Christ alone can give this knowledge, and assure of this love, for He is " God manifest in the flesh "—the incarnate Saviour. He came "*from* the bosom of the Father," and was also "*in* the bosom of the Father," speaking the truth concerning the Father, shewing us unmistakably the mind and heart of the Father. Remember, that if Christ spoke not with authority, no one else has. Who can tell us of God? Where is there any revelation outside the Bible? Our own hearts, unless guided by the light of that word, might lead us astray. We might have thought only of His unswerving justice, and have been ignorant of His love. But it is love,—knowledge of divine love that we need. Christ reveals this. He tells us that " God so loved the world that whosoever believeth in Him might not perish but have everlasting life."

Faith in love is life ; doubt is death. Let the son doubt his father, or the parent a child ; let the husband doubt the wife, or a wife her husband, and what misery will then cloud the soul ! Perfect confidence is life. Now this is what we want towards God. And "this is the confidence that we have in Him," that if we believe we are pardoned, and if we ask anything of Him it shall be done. A pardoning, a prayer-hearing God, is revealed by Christ. This is the well of life opened up in the Bible.

We may drink *freely* of the well. Some, who would have us draw from the vain cisterns of priestly reserve, warn us from going to the Scriptures and to Christ for ourselves. Says Dr. Pusey, " We acknowledge Holy Scripture to be the source of all saving truth, but it does not follow that everyone, unguided, is to draw water out of that living well." That which God has left to all is not to be reserved for a few. Draw all ; draw freely.

In the east, the figure used by Christ would be more appreciated than it can be in our island home, where springs and wells and rivers abound, where the face of nature is ever green, and the landscape so cultivated, that, as one has said, " it seems to have been mapped out, not with spade or plough, but drawn with a pencil." Still we can, amid the heat and feverishness of modern western life, feel, perhaps, more strongly than the orientals, the need for a Christ to satisfy the soul, to sustain in life's toils, journeys, sufferings, sorrows and bereavements.

If it were permitted to man to select the liquid which should best assuage the thirst of all dwellers on earth, what one liquid could be put in the place of water ? There are men who can live without ever tasting simple water, but the mass of human kind could not so exist. Equally adapted to the lips of the child and those of the adult, is simple water. So in Christ, and in Christ only, are the plain truths of God's mercy and love made known. In Christ we see how God redeems; how He is willing to bless; how He is even anxious for our love; and how He is ever ready to sustain us with His strength. Christ is the one for whom the best of all ages had thirsted. He is the one who answers all heart-longings, and upholds in all life-trials. He it is who heals our sins' diseases, delivers from death's sting, proclaims our forgiveness, and announces our future happiness in the world of glory. In Him we see what God wishes to be to us, and what a holy God would have us be to Him. In Him we get our first draught of the river of the water of life. Truly that which Christ gives is unique in its character, both because nothing can supply its place, and because it is given only by Christ.

Now let us see what *unfailing freshness* is brought into our lives by Christ. He is ever moving us to newer life. Water is constantly moving. "It sails above us in fleecy cloud, or wraps us in vapoury mantle; it descends in the gentle shower, or rises in the summer dew; it sweeps along in the pelting storm, or silently works underground to feed the springs; it leaps to our lips from the fount in the rock, or the spring by the roadside." It dashes past us in the mountain torrent, or flows gently by in the reed-fringed and tree-shaded river; it forms itself into huge liquid mirrors in our meadows, or at the foot of mountains, and it spreads round the globe as the wavy-robe of ocean. By constant movement it maintains its freshness; by its rising to heaven and descending on earth, it keeps up incessant circles of blessing. Thus with the truth of Christ when received into the heart; it is constantly moving to some higher aim, and by leading us to effort maintains the spiritual vitality and freshness.

Not only does water nourish the tender herb of the field, and the physical frame of man, but by its continued flow it wears the rocks and changes the face of nature. So Christ's truth is *always* working to wear away imperfections of character and failings of spirit. It will work until the whole nature shall be renewed and brought into conformity to the will of God.

Now this constant stimulus to growth in character, in holiness, in aspirations, is in itself an immense boon. How frightful a thing it is for a man to lose all hope of improving in his moral nature, and so of increasing in knowledge of God! The man must stagnate and become corrupt who has no impelling principle of Christian truth and love working in his soul. But if he has drunk deeply of the water of life which Christ gives, there will be an unfailing spring of freshness in his soul—"a well of water springing up into everlasting life." Christ not only produces and sustains life, but "enters into the secret place of the soul, whence the desires spring, and makes that a living well."

What a number of things there are in the world professing to be well-springs of life and satisfaction! They seem to say, "Whosoever drinketh of the cup we offer shall have all desires gratified." Men hasten to quaff the cup which pleasure holds so enticingly out; or to grasp the golden rewards of business; or to seek honour, renown, power. Each in turn proves unsatisfactory. For a short time there may be some delight arising from the rest from effort and knowledge of possession or attainment, but it soon palls. The universal experience of men is, that nothing but Christ in the world can really satisfy the higher longings of the soul. Where the conscience is deadened and the soul-voices silenced, the reward and pleasure of possession gained may appear to satisfy; but where the mind and heart, the conscience and soul are active, they cry out for a living water to satisfy; they turn from the cup which the world offers with every sign of disgust. That which was to have been the water of life and wine of gladness proves to be but as the "vinegar mingled with myrrh and gall" which was offered to the Saviour. Sour, stupefying, nauseous draught, shall they drink thereof? Taste it they may; drink of it, no! When Christ tasted thereof He would *not drink.* Let His example on the cross be our example in the world.

Although we thus speak we know that many will not believe that the world cannot offer that

unfailing freshness which Christ gives. If in
former pursuits they have been disappointed at
results, they will yet think that the fault lay
in the fact that they had chosen a wrong time
for the effort, or wrong object, or that certain
conditions were lacking which in the future would
be present and propitious. Hence they go from
place to place, hurry from country to town, and
from town to country. Now they are at the sea-
side, anon they are up the mountains; now they
are seeking to cross oceans in yachts, or con-
tinents on foot. They seek endless amusements,
varied society, most exciting books, and the
most thrilling news, anything and everything
that may have in it a dash of freshness,
something to break the *ennui,*—the staleness
and flatness of existence,—something to strike
a fresh well-spring of joy. Many, like the
woman of Samaria, to whom Christ addressed
the words of the text, turn from the lawful
and seek in an *unlawful* style of life the draughts
of joy for which they pine. They, like her,
sink, and must sink, lower and lower by the
effort. Out of empty cisterns they strive to
draw water. By the sea shore of selfishness and
indulgence they dig wells, and the water instead of being the "water of life," is corrupt,
brackish, and salt. It only aggravates thirst.
"Whosoever drinketh of this water shall thirst
again," but whoso drinketh of the water that
Christ shall give him shall never thirst, but that
water shall become a well of freshness.

The Christian, however, has a constant freshness in this life. He has through Christ new hopes, new aims, a new object of faith and of love, and a new friend in all his joys and sorrows. He also has a new object of study. In the Bible he searches for more and more knowledge of Christ and of salvation. Daily he finds by prayer fresh power to overcome sin, and a fresh incentive to increased humility, purity, and charity. Christ's love springs up in his heart, and becomes an ever-flowing stream of love to others. This finds expression in effort. New occupations are thus found. Spiritual work in the church or prayer meeting, and especially in the Sabbath school or visitation of the suffering will be found. He will have great joy—constantly renewed joy—as he unites with others in Sabbath praise. Sunday after Sunday his feet tread with gladness the sacred courts, and never does he tire of those sweet hymns that express the desires of his soul.

> "The men of grace have found
> Glory begun below."

Christ thus freshens and enlarges our being. The single draught of love received at that moment, when beneath the cross we first realized that we were pardoned and accepted in Him, has become a well of the water of life, "springing up into everlasting life."

In order to *maintain this freshness* we must *keep near to Christ.* The well must be constantly *refilled* by Him. All "our springs" must be in Him. We must be careful not to allow the well to run dry through neglect. The more we draw out, the fresher and fuller it will remain. Wells can easily be spoiled by some fetid pool, or foul drain, or polluted river running near. So this freshness of life in Christ may be spoiled by contact with persons of low moral aims, or by entrance into circumstances of questionable character. Our lives may be easily tinged by other things than those that foster purity and peace.

In Devonshire, where water filters through reddish soil, the wells and brooks are of a reddish character. In other places they are of a brownish colour, from the peaty nature of the soil. Few Christians pass through the world without thus receiving some discolouration of their spiritual life. The society in which they mingle, or the circumstances of temptation in which they at times are placed, cause the discolouration. Very watchful must all be who would keep themselves pure unto the end. See how even a favoured disciple, like Peter, when he neglected the warning of Christ and went and stood as one with the enemies of Christ, spoiled and fouled the well-spring of his faith and love by the dastardliness of his denial, and cowardliness of his cursing. Not until he penitently came back to Christ was the spring of life cleansed. Then did " his words become as deep waters, and the well-spring of wisdom as a flowing brook."

In order, also, to maintain this freshness, *knowledge must keep pace with emotion.* It is not enough that we come to Christ and drink of the well-spring of love, but we must grow in grace and knowledge. We must have light. Most visitors to Niagara, after having gazed on the mighty cataract, go some little distance up the Canadian side to a spot where they are shewn a well of light. Entering a dark room, and by the feeble glimmer of a candle we peer down into the well. We can see nothing, but we can hear the plash of a pebble thrown into the water. While we stand there the attendant throws in a lighted match, and now the whole surface of the well was in a blaze. We heard that in some parts of the States, men, by means of pipes, conducted the fumes from these wells into their dwellings to serve as light in the winter nights. What a suggestion for us! If we only grow in knowledge of Christ, we shall not only have ever-freshness of life, but a well of light also. Oh, what we owe to Christ for life and light and love. How we should praise Him! Isaac was praised for the wells he dug, — Esek, Sitnah, and Rehoboth, which names mean Envy, Contention, and Room,— and Christ surely deserves praise, for He hath delivered us from envy of spirit, the contention of Satan, and brought us a great joy.

Jacob's name was handed down with honour to the time when Jesus spoke with the woman of Samaria; and even to the present, because of

the well he dug near Sychar. And Christ hath
opened a well of love and salvation at the gate
of every life. The Emperor Claudius carried
the fresh water of the mountains by an aqueduct over the marshy Campagna into the city
of Rome. That grand aqueduct is now broken
and useless. The arches stand out, here and
there, boldly against the dreary landscape ;
but dilapidated and spoiled as the aqueduct
now is, Claudius has gained more glory by
his beneficent work than others by the
victories they won. And our Saviour has
brought the bright stream of heavenly love
over the marshy campagna of our sin, to cheer,
to cleanse, to renew our souls, and no lapse of
time can ever render His work useless or break
down its power.

In the reign of James I., a nobleman sought
to bring the springs of Hertfordshire into the
heart of Islington. It was for this man, single-
handed, a great undertaking. Many were the
difficulties he had to overcome. Engineering
skill had not reached such a point of power at
that day as this. To lead the channel of the New
River over valleys, round hillsides, through strata
of very porous nature, was no easy task. Sir
Hugh Myddleton spent the whole of his large
fortune in the undertaking, and after many
vexatious delays and disappointments, he had
the pleasure of seeing success attend his efforts.
The water only waited the breaking down of
one barrier to burst in and fill the large

cistern prepared for it. "This was done with ceremony," says a chronicler of that period. "A troop of labourers, in gay apparel, with various implements, came in and marched three times round the cistern, in presence of the mayor and a large company of citizens; then at the utterance of certain words the barrier was burst, the flood gates flew open, the stream ran gallantly into the cistern. Then the drums were beaten, and the trumpets sounded their triumphal tones, while the bells of the city gave forth brave peals and chimes." In the centre of the district stands a statue in honour of the nobleman who conferred so great a boon on his fellows. Many a time I passed it, ere I understood why it was raised. What tribute shall we raise to our Saviour, who has not only brought life and immortality to light, not only given us hope, but has given us a life that is to spring up into everlasting life. We cannot realize yet how much we owe to Him. When we reach the other world, all our present delight and constant freshness of life in Christ will be seen to have been only hints, faint hints of the glory. When we put off mortality and "put on immortality;" when the flood gates of eternal glory shall fly up, and heaven's hosts shall welcome us; when the trumpets shall sound, and we shall be changed; when the bells of the city shall be set ringing, and all its innumerable throngs shall rejoice, that through Christ, we, as blood-bought souls, have been brought safe into heaven, then shall we begin to understand something of what we owe to Christ for His unique and ever-freshening gift. If Isaac, and Jacob, and other benefactors receive honour, surely to Christ shall endless praise be given and glory ascribed.

"Springing up *into* everlasting life," means that this spiritual life, given by Christ, is not only divine in its source, but eternal in duration. We are to dwell with Christ for ever. Our existence is to be typified by that river of life, on either side of which stand the trees of life, whose leaves are for the healing of the nations. There is to be deep-flowing devotion combined with fruitfulness and healing power. We shall have some means of still glorifying God. Not until we reach the other world, and gaze on that river,—over which will never hang the mists of sin, and whose glassy surface will never be stirred by the gusts of passion ; that river, by the side of which will wander the hosts of the redeemed, robed in whiteness, and led by the Saviour,—shall we know the meaning of the words, "springing up into everlasting life." Every zephyr that floats over that river, will bear to our happy spirits, as its burden of joy, the words, " For ever ; for ever."

But if that joy is to be ours, we must be in Christ now. We must be united here to Him by a living faith and fervent love. O ye who are seated by the bitter waters of the world ;

ye who have been vainly striving to satisfy your souls from its empty wells ; ye whose hearts are bitter at the memory of endless disappointments, sorrows, or bereavements.—will you not come to Christ ? He could change, renew, purify, cleanse your souls, and give eternal peace. Shall it be done for you ? It seems, perhaps, hopeless. Thus it once seemed hopeless that some lakes in the midst of the Egyptian desert, called the Bitter Lakes, should be purified. None could drink of them. At length Lesseps turned the waters of purity into them. Bitter Lakes have become waters of sweetness. Shall not something like this be done for you ? Christ is able to do that which seems impossible. At great cost, even the sacrifice of Himself, he does it. Open your hearts. Yield to the Holy Spirit. Come to the living fountain. Come ere you perish. Come pining and panting, and Christ shall give thee life. Come away from the reedy, stagnant, slime-covered pool of thy pride and self-righteousness. Come and drink deep of Christ's love as it flows purling and splashing by, bearing life to thousands. Come, for this water of life is provided without money and without price. Reject it, and where shall we ever find even one drop to cool our fevered tongues ? I linger as one who has been digging and seeking to find water, but who cannot strike a spring. We would stir souls to seek Christ. We would even make a personal appeal to thee, O reader, if un-renewed, and would say, " Believe on the

Lord Jesus Christ and thou shalt be saved;"
yea thou shalt drink of salvation, and never
thirst again; but a well of water, of constant
freshness, shall be in thee here, and spring up
into everlasting life beyond.

THE SYNAGOGUE BUILDER;
OR, THE UNWORTHIEST THE WORTHIEST.

SCRIPTURE REFERENCE—*Luke* vii. 7—9.

SERVICE is at this day too frequently rendered to employers for payment rather than from preference. The outward relationship of employer and employed may be maintained with strict justice on both hands, but no further bond of union be formed than that which has a value that can be measured in gold or silver. It may have been very much the same when the centurion, of whom this passage speaks, lived, but at any rate the value he set on his servant was not measured by money. A relationship was kept up outwardly of master and man, but there was an inward affection on the part of each. This was the more remarkable in a day when service was chiefly rendered by slaves. In the Roman Empire at that day a servant was but a chattel, but this Roman centurion looked upon his as a friend. We are not certain that this servant

was a purchased slave ; he may have been. It
is probable that he was a personal attendant to
this military officer, but not an "orderly," or
soldier detailed for service. The word (παις)
might be understood in the sense of valet, boy,
or child. It is the same as in *Acts* iv. 30
where it is rendered "child."

We are told in the second verse that this
servant was "dear" unto his master. It is
pleasant to read of such attachment on the part
of the master, and to see his solicitude on behalf
of his servant. Doubtless the attachment was
reciprocal. That servant probably thought that
there never was such a good master.

We have heard masters speak of their servants
in tones of affection, and we have seen servants
weep at the remembrance of good and pious
masters.

How touching is that incident recorded of
Oberlin's servant, who was found weeping one
day, and on enquiry being made by Oberlin as
to the cause, was told "I am sorrowing because
I am afraid that in heaven I shall not be able to
serve and wait upon you as here."

In order to create such attachments there
must be, on the part of a master, generosity and
confidence, on the part of the servant, trust-
worthiness and devotedness.

We have, at the first glance, something that
speaks highly of the character of the centurion.
It was well known how attached he was to his
servant. Now that he is taken ill, and either

lying on the couch shaking with palsy, or rolling in the agonies of deadly Syrian fever, his master does all he can for him ; and that, not merely because of the value of his services, but for the affection that exists between them. All that medical aid could do was probably pressed into use. Rude, however, was the medical skill of that age, and in this case it seemed of no avail. When hope reached the lowest point somebody brings tidings of the approach of Jesus. It would appear that the centurion had heard of Jesus before, knew of His miraculous power and merciful practices. " Most opportune," he says, " I will go to Him and ask Him to come and heal my servant. But stop, I am not worthy to go to Jesus. Would that I had someone to send. Whom can I send ? " And possibly he looks with longing eye through the latticed window adown the narrow street that runs off from the castle garrisoned by his company. As he gazes he catches sight of some of the elders of the synagogue. He thinks that if any have influence with Jesus they will have it.

He goes to them and urges them to undertake his suit. To this they consent. They could not do otherwise for one who professed such admiration for their loved Judæa, and who had even in that city of Capernaum built at his own cost for them a place of worship.

Matthew tells us that the centurion himself *went* to Christ, Luke that he *sent* unto Him. The brevity of the account in Matthew may

indicate why he has thus represented it.
Luke is more copious here. There is simply
an exchange of persons, of which we find many
examples in historic narratives and in daily
life.

It may be that the centurion *"sent"* *and yet*
"went." He keeps in the background and makes
the elders his mouthpiece. When he sees
that Christ is willing to come he hastens home,
and thinking how great the liberty he has taken
sends other friends to say, "Lord, trouble not
thyself, for I am not worthy that Thou shouldest
enter under my roof," and urges them to explain
the reason wherefore he came not himself to ask
this favour. He is overpowered by the condescension of Christ. He is fearful, too, lest he
should have appeared uncourteous, yet he feels
that he is neither worthy to ask nor to receive
the boon he desired. He tells them to say,
" Neither thought I myself worthy to come unto
Thee, but speak the word only and my servant
shall be healed."

See what a *view the centurion had of himself.*
To some, his humility would appear over-strained.
Most men feel themselves worthy enough to
enter any presence and to mingle in any society.
Some think themselves deserving of any kindness and meritorious enough to obtain any mercy.
Some even think themselves righteous enough
to have gained salvation, and that they are
more than worthy. Goethe speaks of a
time when he thought he had even

" made God his debtor." Not so with the centurion. The centurion appears to have had a *deep sense of sinfulness and great longing for peace.* He was a proselyte of the gate. He had renounced idolatry and embraced Judaism. Its monotheistic system was in his sight far more acceptable than the polytheistic religion of his native land. Paganism could give no peace. The multiplicity of Gods only mystified men. The impure character of many only made morality the more questionable. He abjured idolatry and confessed the one invisible Jehovah. He accepted the decalogue as his rule of faith and life. Probably this brought him some peace for a time, and either to prove his gratitude or express his devotion to the God of Israel he erected a synagogue at his own charge in a part of Capernaum that needed such a place of worship.

We cannot tell how much it cost that Roman officer to give up the religion of his fathers and embrace that of a foreign nation. Only a deep sense of need could lead to such action.

We could wish that the same longing might be awakened in the hearts of men who, instead of worshipping a multiplicity of Gods, say that there is no God, or of those who only bow down to worldly self-interests. Such might learn a lesson from the centurion.

The centurion's *view of his unworthiness grew out of his high conception of the worthiness of Christ.* How he had heard of Him we know not. Somehow he has learned to have a high idea of the character of Christ. He may have even mingled in the crowds that at times gathered in the streets and houses of Capernaum to listen to Jesus, or he may have gone down to the sea shore, to watch officially the doings of the multitudes that flocked to the Saviour and were fed by Him. He evidently knew Him to have great power and equal pity.

A Roman would naturally reverence power. His country was an empire founded in force, and the characteristic of his nation was love of power. The Roman officer saw that in Christ there was a power compared with which all the power of arms was nothing. He could multiply loaves of bread for a multitude, whereas this military man knew the difficulties of the commissariat department. This soldier knew that the most he or his nation could do was to direct soldiers hither or thither, order home this legion, order out that ; bid peace take its flight from a province and terror take its place ; but what was all that compared with the power of one who could bid disease depart, or banish the demons, or evil genii whom in his yet half-taught state he imagined to be the authors of the maladies that fell on man.

Reverence for miraculous power however, was not a great thing. It was his idea of the *holiness of Christ's character* that most influenced his view of his own unworthiness. He honoured the orators, philosophers, senators, prætors, consuls, tribunes or emperors under whom he served, but he could not find in them or in any of the men of his nation such purity and disinterested love as in Christ.

This man was not persuaded into believing in Christ. He had come under the influence of Christ's character and could not help being drawn to Him and believing in Him. The effect a knowledge of Christ had upon the centurion, was only to make him feel more his own moral shortcomings and unworthiness.

This is the way that Christ by His Spirit is now convincing the world of sin. He stands as the One only perfectly sinless and self-sacrificing being that has ever trod our earth. Against the bright background of His purity the evil of men's lives is thrown into greater prominence. Men, however, can only see the dark figure of sin when the heart has been trained to estimate the glory of the purity of the Saviour.

To tell a man of his faults may not do him much good, but to point to one who has them not, may stimulate to the effort to get rid of them. Hence to blame men much and insist on their believing immediately the worst of themselves would not lead to such a sense of unworthiness as bringing them under the influence of Jesus and His love. The centurion had in some way come under the influence of Jesus, and learnt enough of Him to make his own unworthiness unbearable in the presence of the Divine purity. This was the centurion's view of himself.

The Saviour's view of the centurion was very high. He regarded him as *worthy of commendation.* He did not fear to praise him. Nor did the Saviour hide the joy He had in being so implicitly believed in. The friend of all, He wishes to get at men's hearts. Any degree of faith in any one He accepts. It is accepted not because He is benefited by it, but because those He loves are benefited and made capable of receiving further blessing. " I have not found so great faith." Ah! here in the least likely person—one whose occupation is the trade of war, Christ finds that which it is His great object to awaken in men, a divine faith. Greater than in all the highly favoured nation Israel was the faith of the Roman centurion. Greater was it than was the faith of any who as yet had been under His immediate training ; greater than some who were afterwards most favoured disciples. Martha said, "Lord, if Thou hadst been here, etc." ; the centurion said, " Lord trouble not Thyself, but speak the word only and my servant shall be healed." As compared with others the centurion's faith was great.

Jesus *does not measure individuals by others, but by themselves.* That is to say, He takes into account the circumstances that have surrounded such. He knew how unfavourable must have been the position of this man for the reception and cherishing of spiritual ideas. His profession was that of a soldier. Soldiers, like sailors, are by their wandering life led into habits of indifference to outward observances of religion or private meditation thereon. The constant subjects of conversation among the centurion's brother officers would most likely be the wearisomeness of life in a province so far from home, the prospects of insurrection among the conquered Jews, or the chances of promotion by the Emperor or his sub-ruler Herod. To rise in favour in the corrupt courts, to have honour and precedence among the men who surrounded ambitious and depraved monarchs, would be the high aim of many : but not so with this centurion ; he would not flatter nor fawn on successful wickedness, but spent his time in gaining knowledge of himself and of divine things. Jesus knew what it cost him to do this in such an atmosphere. Hence He speaks of the faith as great. For one of military rank to be so humble before one who was, humanly speaking, a civilian, was remarkable. Jesus is said to have " marvelled " at it.

Christ accepted whatever of good there was in this centurion. He did not condemn his good works. They were taken as evidences of longing after higher and holier truths, and as exhibitions of that faith which was the most precious part of the man's inner life.

Further, the Saviour granted his request. The centurion, while hoping in Christ, goes in to look on the suffering servant. While he gazes he sees the reddish fever-stricken form change and the shuddering fits cease. Life and health are flowing from Christ into that diseased frame. The coolness and paleness of returned health is felt and seen. The servant looks at his wondering master by his side and then says, "I feel better. Disease fell from me in a moment, strength flowed strongly in upon me. How is it?" The servant knew not what the faith of his master had wrought. One man can be a channel of blessing to another. A vicarious faith is as much a reality as a vicarious sacrifice. Indeed, the former leads to the latter. Jesus would not have become the vicarious sacrifice for man but because He had faith in its effect. "I, if I be lifted up, will draw." So, if men are willing to sacrifice self for others, and have faith, they may bless others. Only Jesus could take away the sin of the world, but each Christian is to seek "to be buried with Christ by baptism into His death," "to be crucified with Christ."—"to fill up that which remains of the sufferings of Christ for his body's sake which is the church," *i.e.*, for suffering fellow man. If only Christian men understood their privilege and power in this respect the world would soon be a different place. They could draw down health and life on this diseased and sin-stricken world even as the centurion did on his servant. Faith is like a spiritual electrical chain in this respect.

The centurion knew not at first how Christ regarded him. He was ignorant of Christ's judgment upon him. Still that judgment was passed, and in the hearing of others. So it is passed on us even now and in the hearing of heaven!

Christ not only approved, and granted the request of the centurion, but *entered* his heart to make His abode for eternity. What condescension! He thought himself unworthy to receive Christ into his house, but Christ is willing not only to enter there but to come into his heart.

We see that God *does not despise* us for even weak faith, and yet He desires the strongest possible.

We see that humble faith is a *most appropriate state* for us who come seeking blessings from God. This is the sure way to obtain them. Coming in such a frame and trusting in Jesus we have that which we desired.

We see, too, that any other state than that of humility unfits for the reception of the blessing.

Suppose he had spoken proudly of his high military position, of the success he had had in life, of the bravery he had exhibited in war, of the leniency he had shewn to the wounded or prisoners, or of his generosity in building a place of worship in Capernaum for men not of his nation, or of his great kindness to this servant who was now ill, would these have availed to obtain the desired boon?

Yet how we hear men boast of their "not being so bad as others," of their "having been brought up religiously," "having gone to Sunday school," of their having had good parents, or of their doings, and that they are good masters, or honest men, or that they give liberally to this church or that society. Is that the state in which to gain spiritual blessing for ourselves or for others? Pride must go. It is like poison in the chalice of our prayers. We must fling away pride or it will hurl us from eternal life and joy.

The most fruitful bough bends lowest. The ship most richly and heavily laden sinks deepest in the water. So a strong but humble faith bears the richest blessings to ourselves and others, but pride is as a sunken rock on which the whole may be shattered and sink out of sight.

We see, too, that we must *not be proud of humility.* That is another pitfall into which we might slip. Moses was the most favoured man spiritually ; his face shone with inner glory of holiness, but he was also the meekest of men.

On the other hand, we are *not to be so humble as not to take God's word* implicitly. Some are too humble even to confess how much they owe to Christ. They are afraid that if they were to shew their gratitude to Him they would be accounted proud and as professing more than others.

We learn, then, that humility and faith are not the ground of salvation. Christ alone is our salvation ; Christ formed in us the hope of glory.

None could blot out his sin by the merit of faith or humility, the mercy of God alone does that through the blood of the everlasting covenant. We are forgiven for Christ's sake. Not one is in heaven by his own merit. Not one will ever gain it by his own power. We are redeemed by Christ. The feeling of love to Him for the redemption wrought is that which will bind us to the throne of God for ever.

We learn, too, that while *seeking advantage disinterestedly for others, great blessing may come to ourselves.* The centurion gained spiritual encouragement and a Saviour's approval, and the servant gained restored health and possibly also, through the request of his master, spiritual life.

This is the first heathen healed by Christ, and healed at a distance. We see here, a hint that more have faith than are known to the church. They are known to God. Many such will rise up and condemn us who have had such great privileges. Many who have had few religious advantages will yet find their way into heaven, while many whom we expected to meet will be absent. Many a poor fellow who struggled with poverty, hunger, doubt, and despair, but who had a feeble glimmer of faith in the Divine Jesus will be there, while many who passed for respectable Christians here will be *outside.* Many a poor heart-broken deceived daughter of Eve from whom her sisters in silken chastity would have shrunk, will there be seen washing the Saviour's feet with tears of joy, while the selfish and hard patterns of virtue will be *outside.*

From East and West they shall come, a great multitude. This hope it was that sustained Christ. He shall see of the travail of His soul and be satisfied. The agony He endured to save shall have its ample recompense.

And this shall be brought about by the faith of each. The influence of good and faithful men is contagious. Many would hear of what the centurion had done and the faith he had exercised and be stimulated to go and do likewise. It may be that that other centurion who confessed that Jesus, when He hung dying on the cross, was the Son of God, had been led to think about Christ long before he came to this conclusion and confession. It may be also that Cornelius, another centurion, was stimulated by what he had heard of the doings and faith of an officer in the same service if in another legion, to that almsgiving and those good works which came up for remembrance before God. Have our doings any such effect? Is any good influence going forth from us by reason of our faith in Christ?

MALCHUS, THE LAST HEALED.

SCRIPTURE REFERENCE—*Luke* xxii. 51.

ALL four evangelists mention the smiting off the ear of Malchus, but Luke alone speaks of the healing. From John only we learn the names of the smiter and the smitten. Possibly the earlier evangelists hesitated to mention the name of Peter, lest his influence should be weakened; and John only speaks of it that the glory of Christ might thereby be advanced. Moreover, as John was known in the palace of the high priest, he was in a better position to ascertain the name of the high priest's servant. The consistency of the sacred narrative is seen in this fact. It was also just like a Peter to give such a sharp, impulsive stroke; and it would be characteristic of Luke, a physician, to notice the startling fact of the miraculous restoration of a lost member of the body.

How readily the Saviour repaired the damage caused by the mistaken zeal of His servants!

Peter misunderstood Christ's words, "He that hath no sword, let him sell his garment and buy one." The words were to be understood in a spiritual sense. Christ indicated how severe would be the struggle through which His truth would have to pass ere it should gain full power. His servants would have to be as soldiers. When Christ said, "It is enough," it would indicate—although Peter saw it not—that the Saviour was pained, that after all His teaching, His servant should have so misunderstood Him. Peter's obtuseness was in harmony with the carnal ideas that led him afterwards, when he saw his Master stooping to the violence of men, to imagine that his single arm would be more powerful than the brave submission, or the single word of Christ. He knew not the mighty power of the Divine love and forbearance. He had lost his faith in Christ's power to defend Himself, or summon to His aid the angels who ever ministered unto Him. Hence, when he saw his Master taken and about to be bound, he could bear it no longer. "Shall we smite?" is followed by the leaping of the sword from the scabbard. The imprudent act overtakes immediately an inconsiderate question. Zeal outruns wisdom. The fisherman turns soldier, but his untrained hand cannot accurately guide the weapon. With vigour he swoops it round, aiming a deadly blow at the head of the one nearest to him, but just missing that, he lops off the ear of Malchus. As

15

blood is flowing, Christ knows that there will speedily be a *mêlée*, and apart from His supernatural defence,—His poor weak disciples will be as lambs slaughtered by the strong men of the band. Should those who were to be the heralds of His truth be cut off, His great work would be checked. Noticing, therefore, the angry glances and menacing attitudes of the force, He immediately seeks to check the mischief, and repair the damage caused by His ardent and mistaken disciple. He said, "Suffer ye thus far," which meant. "bear with the over-zeal of My servants," or, "unloose Me, that for a moment I may repair just this slight damage." Then, turning to Peter, He said, "Put up thy sword into its place; all they that take the sword shall perish with the sword." Peter was not blamed by Christ so much for his zeal as rebuked for his want of faith. Christ knew that it was the offspring of a just anger, and that the brave though weak defence was better than retreat. Alas, it is to be feared that he was striking as much to keep up his courage as to defend his master. Anyhow, what a contrast, his fitfulness, impetuosity, and miscalculated strength presents to the calmness and majesty of Jesus, even when in the hands of sinners. Jesus was free, though bound; strong, though submissive. He knew that violence would not serve the best interests of His kingdom, but that suffering was better than striking.

Peter's was not the last wound that has been inflicted on the heart of Christ by His disciples. There has been much carnal and mistaken zeal displayed during the past ages of the Church, and much damage has been done in the name, but not in the spirit, of Christ. The Crusaders, for instance, were fired ofttimes as much by love of travel, display, military parade, jealousy, and conquest, as love of Christ. At first, a truly pious enthusiasm stirred them to seek to rescue the Holy Sepulchre, but it was much easier to attempt to do this than to conquer their own passions,—to seek to expiate sin by the use of the sword than by trusting in the Saviour. The Crusades were in some sense a failure, although just as Christ overruled the impetuous act of Peter, so He allowed that by means of the zeal of the Crusaders should be developed courage and knowledge and national interchange, which would benefit the whole race.

Again, the Papal Inquisition was a great curse, but it was the outgrowth of a zeal for the Church and for exactitude of faith. They hunted, watched ; hailed to prison, tortured, slew, and burnt those who were suspected. They sought to advance religion, and did infinite damage to Christianity in the eyes of the world. France is infidel to-day, partly through the excessive restrictions, priestly pretensions, and bitter intolerance of the Papacy as represented by the Inquisition.

Again, sectarianism is a lamentable fact ; but where it exists for spread of truth, or to protest against a widespread error, it is necessary. Much sectarianism is, alas, kept up only because we are jealous of our reputation, rather than anxious for the spread of truth. How unwilling ofttimes are men of different opinions to put themselves in the place of others! How much bigotry has thus spread, instead of the charity that suffereth long and is kind! How often have the conscientious objections of men been represented as mean and unimportant and narrow, when they have been the offspring of fealty to the truth! Thus has a misguided zeal and perverted mind aimed deadly blows at others, paining the Saviour and damaging His cause, tearing His seamless robe, and piercing His heart with worse than Roman soldiers' spears.

But in all these things we believe that Christ has made allowance for human weakness. He has often to make allowance for those things, which, as individuals, we do. The preacher knows that he blunders in the presentation of truth. Parents know that they may err in methods of training, and Christian men in methods of working. Somehow, Christ overrules. When we, like Peter, lose sight of Him, He keeps us in view. In every way He seeks to correct mistakes, repair damage, and increase confidence in Himself. Could we not believe this, some who know that they have erred in one point or another would utterly despair. But we serve One who " knoweth our frame, and remembereth that we are dust."

We see further in this miraculous act of healing, that Christ *blesses even His enemies while manifesting intensest opposition.* Malchus was a servant of the high priest, perhaps a confidant, a trusted spy, a whispering instigator of the assault on Christ. Peter may have caught sight of him as a leader, one who was in the forefront manifesting the greatest bitterness against Christ. Malchus, hearing his priestly master speaking contemptuously of Christ, would catch his manner and spirit. Hence, if Peter's eye caught sight of a leering bitter countenance, there was the quick resolve to have a stroke at him. Whether a quiet observer of events, a secret sympathizer, or an active opponent, we know not, but Jesus at once heals him. Although the loss of the ear would have been only disfigurement, Christ pities him. Hence, disengaging Himself from those who held Him, He touched and healed the ear.

This was the first blow struck by a disciple of Christ. He would have no blow in His defence, as He would have no fire called down from heaven, hence He extended His mercy at once to a wounded enemy.

Christ would teach us also that in doing good, *the need is the claim.* On this principle He acted towards those outside Judaism.—to the daughter of the Syrophœnician woman, the servant of the

Roman centurion, the Samaritan leper, and the demoniac of Gadara. Here, at a time when it would have appeared that He had more than enough to think of, He shows His care and mercy, and performs for an enemy His *last personal miracle*, even as He afterwards offered His last prayer for those who were His immediate murderers.

Of Malchus we hear nothing further. He may have been grateful and have become a disciple, but this is not mentioned. Had he expressed his thankfulness, we believe it would have been mentioned. Certainly he put forth no effort to defend Christ. We fear he was a prejudiced Jew and hardened ingrate. His name probably means " kingly," but the silence of the sacred narrative would indicate that his nature answered not to his name. Malchus is of interest to us only as being the *last* man on whom Christ exercised His healing power.

THE ROMAN PROCURATOR'S WIFE; OR

WITNESS AND WARNING.

Scripture Reference—*Matt.* xxvii. 19.

DIRECT mention of Pilate's wife and her message is only made by Matthew. Someone who was near to the governor when the message was delivered to the prætor may have overheard it and reported it to the disciples. It would be a matter of surprise to them. Pilate must have known how the Sanhedrim regarded Christ, even before He was given into his hands. He knew that they envied Christ; he knew that they had sought to entrap Him. The band of men who went to Gethsemane with Judas would not go without Pilate's knowledge or without his sanction. He must have heard often of that wonderful man of Galilee, who wrought so many miracles. He must have kept himself acquainted with the doings of one who might be dangerous to the continuance of the Roman domination in Judæa. He would doubtless speak to his wife of the

Nazarene ; or she may have learned much concerning Him from those around her. Her attendants would retail in her palace the subjects of interest in the streets. She may have heard of His entry into Jerusalem, when "the whole city was moved." The court at Cæsarea was anxious to see Jesus, and the palace of the prætor at Jerusalem would not be unconcerned about Him.

We are told by Luke (viii. 3) of several noble women who ministered unto Jesus of their substance. The wife of Pilate may have been among the "many others" spoken of. She may have been a disciple, but had this been the case, we think she would have asked Pilate to release and protect Jesus. Indeed, she seems to have been, by her message, only anxious that her husband should not be involved in that which would bring trouble.

There is a tradition that this woman's name was Procla, or Claudia Procula. It has been surmised, owing to her name, that she belonged to the Claudian race, to which the Emperor Tiberius belonged. It is, however, very uncertain as to whether she was of noble birth. She may have been of high station, and through her, Pilate may have received his promotion as governor of Judæa. There is a further tradition that she became a proselyte to the Jewish faith. This is not unlikely. Coming with her husband from Italy, she would naturally be struck with the contrast presented by the simple mono-

theistic worship of the Jews, to the polytheistic
worship of her own land. Into the courts of
the Temple she would doubtless wander. She
would gaze on the imposing ceremonials from
the court of the Gentiles, or view the devout
joyousness of the myriads who came up to keep
the various feasts. To her the Rabbis and
Pharisees would appear as men anxious to be
truly religious. She would long after a pure
faith, but whether she attached herself to Judaism, or became a disciple of the Nazarene, we
know not. In the Greek church she has been
accounted a Christian and canonized as a saint.
It is possible that she had been hesitating, up
to the time of sending the message to Pilate, as
to avowing herself a follower of the despised
Nazarene. Now that Christ is in trouble, she
hesitates no longer. Her dream may have been
the outcome of her waking anxieties. Hence
she took upon her to send to her husband a
remarkable message: " Have thou nothing to do
with that just man, for I have suffered many
things this day in a dream because of Him."
(Matt. xxvii. 19.) Any judge sitting to try a
criminal case at this day would be rather stag-
gered at receiving such a message from a wife.
The administration of law was, at that day,
under the Roman power, almost as punctilious
and dignified as amongst us, and this makes us
regard the message as the more remarkable.

But the *testimony in the message* was not less
remarkable. She spoke of Jesus as " that just

man ;"—righteous as well as innocent. And this was Christ's character before men. Every possible perfection was centred in Jesus. Men maligned Him; said He was a "Samaritan," "had a devil," "was mad." They said that He was a deceiver, impostor, perverter, agitator. They preferred a murderer before Him. They sought His death. They excommunicated Him. They gave command that He should be seized as a dangerous person. They procured soldiers to take Him. They made a great clamouring in the Judgment-hall for His death. Chief priests, and the respectable religious partisans of His day moved the mob to cry "Crucify Him." They deemed Him unworthy to breathe. Thus many regarded Him; but Procla calls Him "that just man." Jewish priests condemned, His own friends forsook Him, the populace demanded His life, but Italia's daughter at that moment testifies to His innocency, worthiness and righteousness.

The testimony was *unexpected.* It was from one of pagan training, but travelled knowledge. It was given *openly.* Others were made aware of her belief. We have only to read the four brief biographies of Christ to be assured that Procla's estimate of Him was right. The character of Christ shines brighter and brighter as the years go by. He is seen to be above man, while associated with man. Sceptics confess to the grandeur and purity of His character. Indeed, like the sun rising bril-

liantly and moving steadily over the firmament, undulled, unclouded, unspotted, so
the character of Jesus has been draw-
ing more and more attention from the
world, and is to-day unquestionably more
honoured than ever before.

The remarkable testimony was also a *wifely
warning*. If Christ were a just man the judge
had better not risk condemning Him. Procla
trembled at her husband incurring the guilt of
such an act. She may have hesitated to inter-
rupt him in the exercise of judicial functions.
Would he not resent such an interference? It
was a daring thing to send to Pilate at such a
moment. She could not but know that the home
authorities objected to governors taking their
wives with them, lest they should make their
husbands too tender-hearted and merciful. She
knew that Pilate had brought her with him
contrary to law, and shall she meddle with his
administration of law? It was a bold act; but
what will not a faithful wife risk for her husband
or children? And the wife of a public man has
often greater anxieties than he has himself.
The mutual confidence and affection between
Pilate and Procla enabled her to risk sending
him the needed warning.

That wifely warning was the outcome of *a
remarkable dream*. We know not whether it
was at night-time or during a morning siesta
that it came. We are not told whether it was
sent specially by God or not. A great French

artist has depicted Procla in the act of descending the palace stairway as a somnambulist, and pausing half-way down, while an angel brings before her mind the vision of the crucifixion and of the glorification of Christ. The face of Jesus she cannot forget. The sufferings of Jesus she foresees and pities. She knows the bitter agony other condemned ones had endured. She may have been one of those noble women who prepared the drugged wine to soften the sufferings of those "ready to perish." She may have heard the tramping of those crowds in the streets when they brought Christ up from the valley of the Kedron to the chief priest's palace ; and again when they led Him to the Judgment-hall. Then falling asleep she dreams of the result. Her dream was doubtless but the outcome of waking thoughts. Anyhow she was assured that her strange dream was of supernatural character. She takes it as a warning from God.

Some have thought that the dream was sent by the enemy of souls, so that Pilate's wife might thus hinder the offering of the atoning sacrifice ; but it appears to have been really a warning by a vision sent to the representative of the Gentiles, even as Jesus, by His own words, had given warning to the Jews.

We have often strange thoughts in dreams. Our greatest poet says of them—

" Dreams
Are the children of an idle brain,

> Begot of nothing but vain fantasy,
> Which is as thin of substance as the air,
> And more inconstant than the wind."

But dreams have often had great power over the life. They give us glimpses of something beyond our ordinary conception, and stir the desires after a holier state. As Henry Vaughan sings:—

> " And yet as angels in some brighter dreams
>   Call to the soul when man doth sleep,
>   So some strange thoughts transcend our wonted dreams,
>   And unto glory peep."

Procla peeped into the unseen, and she " suffered many things." She was pained for Christ and for her wedded lord. She took the dream as a warning to him and to herself.

The warning came at the *most critical moment*. It was greatly needed. The blackest deed ever witnessed was about to be performed. Pilate was about to sacrifice conscience to expediency, and the holy Christ to a mob excited to frenzy by an unscrupulous and bitter priesthood. He looked upon it as but a slight event in his official life, but it was the *one* important event before which all the other deeds of his life are paled.

How such moments of deepest import come and depart silently and quickly. Happy the man who knows how to seize such moments and act on such warnings and suggestions as those received by Pilate.

The warning *disturbed* the judge. Sceptic

as he was, he yet feared the unseen. This may account for the after measures he took to clear himself from participation in priestly guilt. His act was, however, as ineffectual as it was cowardly.

The warning was, alas, *unsuccessful.* The Roman governor acted as though the warning had never been sent, and thus many, also, allow warnings from God's word, good thoughts, and holy influences to pass away unused.

The testimony and warning *increased the prætor's guilt,* and thus the preaching of the gospel to-day, if it saves not the soul, only intensifies its sin. Each one may put himself in the *position* of Pilate, for all must decide as to the claims of Christ. What would be the feelings of Pilate when, after his suicidal death, his soul appeared at the judgment bar? That Christ whom he condemned to crucifixion, between two thieves, now seated on the throne between unnumbered hosts, is his judge. No longer can he silence the voice of conscience. He knows at last his need of the warning and his folly in neglecting it. But his wife had cleared her soul. She had felt pity for Christ, suffered in heart with Him, spoken for Him, and, we believe, must have lived and died for Him.

SIMON THE CYRENIAN;

OR THE COMPANION OF THE CROSS.

SCRIPTURE REFERENCE—*Mark* xv. 21.

OW infrequent is any reference made to Simon the Cyrenian! The denial of Peter, the bitterness of chief priests, the penitence of the thief, and the testimony of Pilate are very often the subject of contemplation, but the cross-bearer's helper is generally overlooked.

It has been thought that Simon the Cyrenian and Simeon Niger, mentioned in Acts xiii. 1, are identical persons. This is uncertain. The Cyrenian may have been a "man of colour." Possibly he was a Jewish colonist who had been settled in Cyrene, or he may have been a native of Libya who had become a proselyte to Judaism. We read of an Ethiopian who studied the Jewish prophets, and who was taught by Philip to believe in Him who was "led as a lamb to the slaughter." Simon has come to Jerusalem either to sell goods or to worship. He has come from a place half way

between Carthage and Alexandria, and must
have had a wearisome journey. We know
not whether he came by the desert, risking
assaults from prowling sons of Ishmael, or by
the clumsy, corn-laden, slave-propelled Roman
galleys that crept along shore by day and
anchored for safety each night. His journey
may have been longer than he had hoped.

Simon passes the night before the passover
in the country, and is just entering the city on
the day of high ceremony, when he meets a
great crowd following three prisoners to execution. The three prisoners bear their crosses. One
of them seems weaker than the others, and falls
under the weight of his cross. While Simon is
scanning the faces of the three condemned men,
and reading in the first hardness and revenge,
in the next some sign of sorrow and regret, and
in the third Divine tenderness, nobility, and
purity, he finds himself seized and compelled to
be the companion of the cross.

Simon knew not how Christ had been all
through life helping others, and how His determination to bless the world made Him need
help at a critical moment. The soldiers in vain
lift up Christ, and try to make Him carry His
cross the rest of the way. Persuasion is vain.
Blows avail not. Someone must assist Him;
but who? Jews were exempt from such indig-
nity as carrying the cross, and the soldiers will
not touch the wood of shame. They impress
the nearest stranger into the work. The dark

complexion of Simon may have drawn attention
to him as an unprejudiced stranger. Anyhow
he was seized and compelled either to assist
Christ in bearing His cross, or to take the whole
weight upon himself.

Where were the disciples at this time?
Where was Peter? Had he been in his place
he might have done from love what Simon had
to do by compulsion.

But *why* was compulsion needed? It may
have interfered with Simon's intentions at the
time. His object may have been to make
money. For this he may have travelled those
many miles, and here he is checked and drawn
into a service for which he has no taste. It
involved somewhat of shame too. The cross
was called "the infamous wood." Whoever
touched it was supposed to be, in a measure,
contaminated. At this day, to cling to the
doctrine of salvation by the vicarious work of
Christ is regarded by some as simply the result
of ignorance and superstition. A cultured man
said to the writer, with much affectation of
surprise, "Why, you are not so foolish as to
suppose that the death of Christ can do anything for you?" It would be comparatively
easy to take up and carry a material cross, but
to bear an active cross of despite and contempt
is more difficult. There are those who are
nominal Christians, who will even wear crosses
as ornaments, but they would shrink from the
cross of definite confession and consecration.

16

Compulsion had to be used because the *effort* to bear the cross of Christ was *not easy*. It had to be carried uphill. It involved pain. It bowed the back. It bruised the shoulder. It stole the breath. Panting and weary, Simon helped to carry it. And every cross means suffering of some kind, in greater or less degree. Some have to bear it when they have to be a burden to others. Thus one with whom we met, said that through ill-treatment she had to go home to be a burden to a parent having already only too little with which to support himself. The cross may take the shape of strong passion, like that of one of our kings who was accustomed to hide himself from others and champ the reeds strewn on the floor, to let off surplus energy and passion, so that in public he might wear a calm face. The cross may take the form of fretfulness or gloominess of disposition, disappointed aims, overpowering ambition, or unforgivingness of spirit, or the fact that in some way we unintentionally injured others ; or that we are cast aside from work—work necessary to support a family, or Christian work in which we delight ; or non-success that has attended prolonged effort ; or great success which only brings increased burdens, the " penalties of greatness." Some have to bear it in losses of wealth or position, or in misplaced confidence, or in misrepresentations which they know they have not deserved, or in a hand-to-hand struggle with doubts on religion, when tormented with sceptical opinions, or swayed by contradictory conclusions. Or they have to bear a black cross when death enters the house and makes lonely the heart,—when a brother or sister, parent, child, wife or husband is taken. To gaze on the vacant chair, to miss the familiar form and face, to "long for the touch of a vanished hand, and the sound of a voice that is still," these things are very heavy crosses, and they have to be borne sooner or later in life.

Christ gave no promise of ease to His disciples. "In the world ye shall have tribulation, but be of good cheer," &c. God intends this to be a state of trial. No class of people can be exempt from trial and suffering. The lofty in rank or abounding in wealth, as well as the obscure and poverty-stricken, the highly-intellectual as well as the ignorant, have to bear some cross or other. The Christian does not expect exemption, but comes to understand that it is necessary for the attainment of that spiritual character and power which God would see developed in us. Paul was doubtless referring to this when he spoke of having fellowship with Christ in His sufferings. Hence, as Simon the Cyrenian was compelled by the soldiers to carry the cross which interfered with his intentions, involved shame and inflicted pain, so we are compelled by circumstances to take our cross and bear it, not uphill to Calvary, but upwards towards heaven.

There were *several counterbalancing advan-*

tages in that cross-bearing. Simon would rejoice afterwards when he came to understand for *whom* he was carrying it. At first Christ was nothing more to him than one of the male-factors, but when he found out that He was the Messiah, the Saviour of the world, the Son of God, he would greatly rejoice.

Further, he had to bear it *after* Jesus ; Christ led the way. He only trod in the footsteps of the Saviour. And every sorrowful heart may remember that Jesus has passed through every-thing that can be a trial, and tasted, yea, drank to the dregs, every cup of bitterness.

Moreover, Christ still *bore part* of the burden. It is possible that the pieces which formed the cross were only connected after arrival at the place of crucifixion. If so Christ may have borne the transverse, and Simon the upright part. Or, if united, Christ may have taken one end—the heaviest—and Simon the other. He always takes the heaviest part of any cross we have to bear, and whatever may bruise our shoulder pains His heart.

There was another thing that counterbalanced any pain in bearing the cross, viz. that *it became a channel of grace* to Simon. It was like a wire along which flashed the electric current of love. Seeing how Jesus bore with patience all His sufferings and only pitied and prayed for His persecutors, Simon could only wonder, admire, love, and adore. That he became a Christian seems probable from the way in which he is spoken of as the father of Alexander and Rufus, evidently well-known men in the Christian Church. It is not unlikely that the reference to the mother of Rufus in Rom. xvi. 13,— "Salute Rufus chosen in the Lord, his mother, and mine," is a reference to the wife of the Cyrenian. And Lucius of Cyrene (Acts xiii. 1) may have been not only a fellow-countryman, but a friend influenced by Simon. To be the means of leading one's family or a friend to Christ would certainly be a great result from bearing the cross after Jesus.

There would be the natural satisfaction of soul also arising from feeling that he had been of use to one in trial. Nor can we imagine that Christ would permit Simon to go away without thanks expressed by word or look, for the assistance—even though compelled assistance— given. What a joy to have been able to do anything for Christ, and to receive His approval. All pain or shame would be nothing after such a reward.

Who would have heard of Simon the Cyrenian but for this incident ? He was afterwards known in the Church as the one who had gone up step by step with Christ to Calvary. His name is written in God's word, and doubtless also in the book of life, for the ages to note and celestial spirits to rejoice over.

How amazed Simon must have been at the results that flowed from that casual meeting with Christ ! How God rewards even constrained service! Little conception could Simon have of what an honour was put upon him in that he was made a companion of the cross, a co-worker with Him who was engaged in the redemption of the world. He carried the altar on which was offered the " Lamb of God that taketh away the sin of the world."

What reasons are suggested from this incident for faith, for a firm trust in God's over-ruling power! Things that seem against us may be for us. "All things work together for good." We believe that God does arrange and control circumstances so that our best spiritual interests shall be served. There are certain laws that roll on, and which might crush our poor hearts, but which are for the best interests of our race. As individuals we may suffer, but our fellows are benefited. The world is not left to manage itself, or go on at haphazard rate. We believe therefore that crosses and trials are all foreseen and overruled. We cannot see at once the Divine intention, but if only true confidence in God is established, that certainly *is* for the best.

We should not, therefore, complain, of the cross, in whatever form it may come. Is it noble, manly, or Christian to wish to bear the least suffering possible—to wish to get to heaven by the smoothest way? Is it noble to let "Jesus bear the cross alone"? Is it noble to rejoice in the benefits of the cross, and to shrink from something of its burden? Is it noble to desire this, when the way is so short, the crown so bright, the reward so great, the glory awaiting us such an "eternal weight"? It is not noble; therefore let us glory in anything that may make us feel more our dependence on Christ, and enable us to enter more into "fellowship with His sufferings," becoming like Simon the Cyrenian, companions of the cross. Those who can cheerfully take up whatever cross may fall to their lot will find that it is only "just such a burden as wings to a bird, or sails to a ship." Thus many have found it. Thus apostles, martyrs, confessors of all ages have found it How many have rejoiced that they were " counted worthy to suffer shame for His name"! Listen to the words of a French Protestant minister imprisoned in a castle in Belgium for his faith. A friend visiting him said she wondered how he was able to eat, drink, or sleep in quiet under such adverse circumstances, when he nobly replied, "Not only can I do all these things, but as for these chains, I esteem them at a higher rate than jewels of gold; their rattling is music in my ears, because it reminds me that I am bound for maintaining the truth of the gospel." That was truly bearing the cross after Christ, in His steps, in His strength, for His glory, and in His spirit. May we all as willingly bear ours, and find jewels in every jeopardy, music in all misery, a strength in every sorrow, and a crown above every cross.

JOSEPH; OR SECRET DISCIPLESHIP.

Scripture Reference—*John* xix. 38.

THE first part of the text is cheering the latter part saddening. Joseph of Arimathæa was a disciple, a believer in and learner of Christ, but he kept it a secret until Christ was dead. He seems not to have attempted to defend Christ before the Sanhedrim. Had he, in conjunction with Gamaliel and Nicodemus lifted up a protest against the proceedings of the chief priests, they would not have been so bold. We are told that he " did not consent to the counsel and deed of them." (Luke xxiii. 51.) He may have been absent from the council which condemned Christ. The rest of the council, suspecting the leanings of Joseph towards the Nazarene, may not have apprised him of their sudden gathering and subtle intentions. Anyhow we hear nothing of his devotion to Christ until it is too late to be of any service, and that which we are told in this passage is not to be understood as spoken in his praise.

Why is it that many who believe on Christ prefer secret attachment to open profession ?

There are different classes of believers in Christ : those who, like Renan, admit the past existence of Christ ; then those who admit his humanity and present existence, but deny His Divinity ; and lastly, those who admit His humanity, Divinity, and present power.

The latter may be attached to Christ's person, word, and work, and yet not confess Him. Why is this ? Possibly it is on account of the stringency of His requirements—humility, child-likeness, purity, simple faith in His atoning work, renunciation of any merit supposed to arise from birth in a certain race included in the covenant of mercy, or merit arising from punctilious observance of the ceremonial law, or effort to fulfil the moral law. Possibly it arises from shame at association with one of such lowly origin, or with one who took so firm a stand against the social and ecclesiastical wrongs of His day. Joseph of Arimathæa would feel the full force of these difficulties.

Some remain secret disciples from fear of being accounted presumptuous for attempting to lead instead of follow ; of being accounted " righteous overmuch ; " of not being able to maintain consistently the profession of the lip. They cannot trust God's grace to keep them from bringing disgrace on Christ's Church. Some remain secret disciples because of wrong and unnatural ideas about religion, or because

of the inconsistencies of some at present professing Christ.

The life of the secret disciple may be even
superior in many respects than that of one professing, but the life is not so noble in this, that it
is passed in acknowledged dependence on Christ.

The one who flatters himself that he is more
consistent than a certain believer must be
watchful lest there should be discovered in
himself much self-righteousness.

Moreover he must remember that the standard
set up for one openly professing is higher than
that of the secret believer. Many are secret
disciples because they do not see the need for
open acknowledgment in order to the sustenta-
tion of public worship, the erection and mainte-
nance of suitable buildings, the selecting of
pastors, of members, and the fostering of all
spiritual work. If no one confessed Christ by
the lip or life, how would His gospel make
progress? To have an objection against a certain form of Church organization must not be
supposed to be a rejection of Christ. If any
have conscientious objections to certain denominations, let them find out one coming nearest to
their conception of primitive Christianity, and
let them join that. If they cannot find any
such as they would like to join, let them state
the reasons for abstinence, and profess still by
the lip and life their attachment to Christ.
Doing this, of course they are no longer secret
disciples, although they are " unattached "
Christians.

The real reason wherefore many remain secret disciples is because there is no fervency of love to Christ such as would lead them to risk anything for His sake. If His love is in the heart, shame, fear, and questions of expediency are hushed, and we can stand for His name before thousands of our fellows or hosts of the redeemed.

The question as to *whether Christ recognized secret discipleship* is a most serious one. Let us see whether we find any hint in the affirmative—in the subsequent history of Joseph. We know little of him. He gave to Him " who had had the death of a malefactor the burial of a King," but in this seems to have had no faith in the promised resurrection. No mention is made of Christ having uttered anything to Joseph like the approval He gave to the woman who " anointed Him to His burial." No mention is made of Joseph's having afterwards met with Christ, or even with the disciples. The tradition of his having come to England and founded the first Church of Christ in this land, at Glastonbury, is only a tradition ; but should it be reliable, it only shows that Joseph had thrown off his secret discipleship. Had his secret discipleship been intentional in order the better to help Christ, as Hushai remained at the court of Absalom the better to serve David ; or as the disguise of Blonde de Nesle as a harper was assumed in order to find Richard Cœur de Leon,—there might possibly be some hope of recognition. Christ is not desirous that we should appear worldly and hide our religion in order to get opportunities of advancing His cause.

There is no suggestion of the recognition of secret discipleship in any of Christ's utterances. He claims absolute open attachment, "following," absence of fear or of shame. " Be not afraid of them that kill," &c. " Whosoever shall be ashamed of Me." " He that is not with Me is against Me." When He said, " He that is not against Me is on My part," He was speaking of one who was an open disciple, but who dissented from the injunctions of the apostles, and probably repudiated their right to forbid his working in the name of Christ.

In the nature of things it must seem most improbable that secret discipleship should be recognized by Christ. If we are ashamed of Him here, we could not be persuaded hereafter that He would not be ashamed of us, even if He had not said that the names of such He would not " confess before His Father and the holy angels." Dare we then seek to be neutrals, or mere secret disciples ? Suppose Christianity is weak ; we ought because it is right to side with it. Suppose it despised ; we ought to remember that Christ makes us rich. Gratitude for what Christ has done and is still doing should lead us to confess Him. Anticipation of the need for His recognition, of which we shall be sensible at last, should lead to confession here.

How painful is the sense of isolation when we find ourselves in some bright gathering, or strange town, without knowledge of a soul therein ; how thankful are we in such case to anyone who, even if unintroduced, speaks a kindly word, leading us to feel at home in a strange place !

Suppose we could even get into heaven in the garb of secret discipleship, should we not be most thankful to anyone who would recognize us ? If only He who is the " Head over all " should notice us, our joy would be beyond bounds, while our shame at our former secret discipleship would be at the same time overwhelming. Can we therefore now withhold from Him who is our best friend, our atoning sacrifice, our Sustainer, our Guide, our King, our God, an implicit devotion and open confession ? Can we bear to think that after death men might speak of any of us as " a disciple of Jesus, but *secretly* for fear ?"

BARABBAS; OR, UNEXPECTED RELEASE.

Scripture Reference.—*Luke* xxiii, 25.

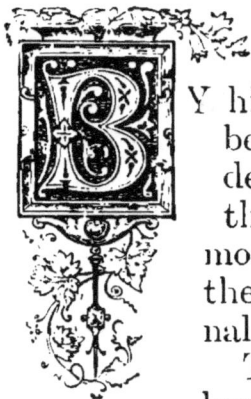

B Y his hesitancy and truckling, Pilate became guilty of a judicial murder. He who should have been the exponent of righteous law acted most unjustly. "Willing to content the people," he set free a real criminal and crucified the Christ.

There is ever great danger in allowing vital questions of truth and justice to be decided by a mob heated by passion. The desire of "the people" was not that of the whole Jewish nation, but only of a bigoted section. Still the priests and the mob represented the nation in this case. The officials, careful for "place and nation," had in secret counsel condemned Jesus to die, whether guilty or innocent. They did not foresee all the difficulties attendant upon compassing the death of Christ. They were afraid that at the last He would slip from their power, and therefore they suggested to the people that, as it was the custom of Pilate to release every year at their

Passover some prisoner, they should ask that he would do as he had always done. Then they suggested a name, that of Barabbas. They would have him rather than Christ.

This releasing of prisoners on certain occasions of joy is one of those practices in which human law is tempered by mercy. In the public press very recently it was recorded that when the new mayor of a certain city took his seat for the first time on the bench, "the first prisoner, being accused of only a slight offence was, in accordance with a time-honoured custom, discharged."

Now when Pilate proposed to release Jesus, he did so because, if there were any accusation against Him, it was but slight. The Jews, however, entreated that not Jesus, but Barabbas, might be granted unto them. They had weighed in their minds the worth of the two, Jesus or Barabbas, and they preferred that Barabbas should live. Think of the blessed Saviour being balanced against a Barabbas. Think of a Barabbas having the opportunity of depressing the beam when it was a question as to which should live.

Think first of *the character of the man who was preferred by the world before Christ.* His name is said (by Origen) to have been Jesus Barabbas. This is equivalent to being the son of a distinguished father, or of a Rabbi. He seems to have been associated with others, and to have been the ringleader in an insurrection.

In this insurrection murder had been committed. Barabbas was taken and condemned. He may have been a fierce desperado, able to play the assassin, as well as to rifle the girdles of those who fell into his power. If his efforts had been against the Roman power, he was a sort of desperate revolutionary. He may, indeed, have been only one of a gang of banditti infesting the gloomy gorge leading to Jericho, ready to strip or leave half dead, or altogether dead, any poor wayfarer. Emboldened with success, he may have carried his operations into the very city. He thinks to enrich himself and his followers, if only he can foment disorder and anarchy among the many who go up to the Passover. He was one of a set, perhaps as bad or worse than himself. It is said of him that he was "of those" who had made insurrection in the city. His plans were, however, frustrated. He was found in the strong grip of the law he had evaded so long. This was the man whose release the Jews demand before that of Christ.

Now we know what was the character of Jesus of Nazareth, who was to die if Barabbas lived. Jesus was the truest, purest, gentlest, most unselfish and loving being that ever trod our earth. He was so merciful that He even performed His last miracle for one of his enemies, and offered His last prayer for murderers. We know that He was more than man, that He was the wondrous being whose advent many prophets and righteous men had desired to see.

He was God manifest in the flesh. He was the Word "by whom all things were created," and "without whom was nothing made which was made." Barabbas owed his life to Him, and yet this Christ is now accounted by the priests and people as being less worthy to exist than Barabbas.

Can we not hear the cries for Christ's crucifixion that resound in that forum of Pilate? Can we not see those priests moving about to incite the people to a more lusty demand for the condemnation of Jesus of Nazareth, and for the release of Barabbas?

What a fearful choice! Horrifying exchange! A profligate before the Prince of Life, an insurrectionist before Immanuel, a robber before the Redeemer, a schemer before the Saviour, a murderer before the Messiah, Jesus the son of Abbas before Jesus the Son of God! This is how the world has ofttimes treated Christ. This also is how many individuals have despised the One who came to seek and to save the lost.

Barabbas had nothing to do with that choice. He was the subject of it. Could we say in the light of the judgment day that we have not lived for self, and sought our own ends? We may not have acted just as he did, by robbing others, but we have sought worldly gain just as earnestly and greedily. We have robbed God of the service and glory we should give Him. We may not have slain others by club or poignard, but have we never slain others with the bitter

17

word or covert insinuation? We have not done overtly that which might be to others a sign of our possession of a similar spirit to that of Barabbas or of the priests, but we may nevertheless have in us the germ of equal evil. Indeed, if all the life were known, and we could see it in the light of God's requirements and Divine holiness, we might find that we had a sort of *brotherhood with Barabbas*, and a part with the prejudiced and perverted priests.

Contemplate the release of Barabbas. Gather the suggestions which should be started thereby. What effect had it upon him? He was condemned and in the firm grip of the law, with no prospect of deliverance. Barabbas saw nothing but the cross before him. We can see him in that cell of his, with the heavy irons on his hands, and the watchful soldier by his side. He expects on the morrow to suffer. The day he expected to be his last has been a long one. The sun throws its last rays into his prison. The brief twilight is gone, and leaves him to the horror of night. He passes it in fitful dreams of the cross. Visions of a wife or of mother who had loved him perhaps come also. Mayhap his wife had striven to see him that day, but had been denied. Possibly he had heard her voice outside entreating entrance, or lifting a bitter wail at the harsh refusal. Barabbas was a man, and however he might have sinned, must have retained some sensibility. Being a Jew, he would know the law and dread the consequences of sin which would follow him into Sheol. The night passes in a troubled way. Ever and anon, when the guard moves, and his greaves or a sword grate upon the hard pavement, Barabbas starts up, thinking it is the blow of the hammer and rattle of the nails that will fasten him to the dreaded cross. But what is that noise in the street? What crowd is that? What soldier-voices? The perspiration stands in beaded drops on his brow. They are coming already for me! No, they were leading up the Via Dolorosa from the garden beyond Kedron the Man of Sorrows, who would be *the substitute for Barabbas.* He hears the soldiers dragging out crosses. "One of them is for me! How many more will die with me!"

The night is not half gone yet. Barabbas briefly sleeps. He is awake again. The day is dawning, he thinks. " Day of my death is this! Day when I must stand before my God."

What is that cry? He hears his own name mentioned. In that "wild liturgy of death" raised by the clamouring multitude around Pilate he can hear the name of BARABBAS taking a prominent place. " They are crying out already for my crucifixion," is his fear. Pale, he asks his keeper the meaning of that sound.

" List, there is the footstep of the soldier come to lead me forth to execution." The massive bolts are withdrawn, and the heavy door, groaning on its hinges, rolls back. Barabbas buries his face in his hands. " Barabbas, by the order of Pilate you are to be released."

" Crucified, you mean!" he says, amazedly.

" No, *released!* Strike off these fetters. Let him go free." His guard obeys. The fetters fall. Barabbas, dazed with the sudden tidings of joy, staggers out of the prison and stands in the narrow street, trying to assure himself that it is not a dream. As he breathes the clear air and listens to the shouts of soldiers in the guard-house, he knows he is free.

Thus there is an illustration of how deliverance comes to the sinful soul ofttimes in the same *unexpected* manner. We are conscious of our danger. We tremble in view of the future. We hear in our consciences the rolling thunder of a threatening law. Deliverance comes through *another, who has died for us.*

Barabbas *cared not* for Christ, *yet Jesus died for him.* Perhaps he would have despised Him as a Nazarene, yet Jesus saved him. He *asked not* for deliverance, yet it was given through another. And we may not have asked to be saved through Christ, yet by His stripes we are healed, by His death set free from the law.

How did he think of Jesus afterwards? Did he see the one who took his place? Possibly, as he emerged from prison, he may have met the crowd and guard leading Jesus to Golgotha. He may have seen Christ fall under the weight of the cross; a cross *intended for himself.* He may have mingled with the crowd, and, the better to shield himself, joined in their rude cries. The more likely act on his part would be to find some place of hiding, lest his release should have been a mistake. Jerusalem would not long be his abiding-place. Outside the walls he will feel safer, and in some cavern he can find a secure hiding-place.

But when night has again come on, has he forgotten the one who died for him? We can imagine him thinking he would go and see the spot where he expected to suffer, and the one who had taken his place.

There is no tradition that he became a convert, but we can suppose that he did go and look on the one who had taken his place. Look at him, a few paces from the cross. The soldiers have gone away to a distance, and Joseph and Nicodemus have not yet come to take Jesus down. Barabbas might gaze in quiet on that dead Christ. What would his thoughts be? "That cross was intended for me. Those cords were to have cut my wrists and limbs. Those nails were to have pierced my hands and feet. Instead of standing here, conscious of life, I might have hung there drooping in death. Or I might have still lingered in thirst and torture, praying for death. He has died for me." We can imagine Barabbas, when the body of Christ was borne to the tomb, following at a distance, with soul awed by the earthquake, the strange darkness, and the dread events of that day. As he looks into that tomb he may have thought,

"He lies there for me." He may have seen that Christ died for his sin, oh, did he learn that Jesus rose again for his justification, for his eternal salvation?

How did Barabbas die? Where? No account remains. But what if the very man who was set free by Christ's bondage, who was spared the cross by Christ's suffering, should never have learnt the deeper truth of spiritual freedom and eternal salvation! Anyhow, if he knew it not before, we believe he would learn that after death. Sooner or later we must learn what Christ has done for us. He hung on that cross as certainly for *each* of us as for Barabbas. What have been our thoughts of our debt to Christ? What have we done to show our gratitude? Have we gone away content that we have a great many privileges and joys through the influence of Christianity, but altogether indifferent as to the personal devotion which should be evoked to Him who died for us?

If Barabbas went away to enjoy himself and carouse with companions over his escape, while Christ went to death, how terrible the thought! How different were the two paths each trod that day! Barabbas congratulated himself that he was not going to the cross, Jesus went there in sorrow; the one, however, went into oblivion; the other to a throne of triumph in the cross of shame.

Now of which would we be followers? Shall

we be glad to be free as Barabbas, or shall we be willing, like Paul, to be crucified with Christ —crucified in our sinful nature, our self-will, our pride, our indifference, our neglect, our prejudice, our self-righteousness? It would be a cowardly thing to rejoice that Christ suffers, unless we have fellowship in those sufferings, and mourned the sins which nailed Him to the tree.

BARNABAS;

OR THE CATHOLIC-SPIRITED DISCIPLE.

SCRIPTURE REFERENCE—*Acts* xi. 24.

BARNABAS is spoken of by Luke as "a good man, full of the Holy Ghost and of faith." His goodness and faith led him to be wide in his sympathies and charitable in his dealings with others. He was unselfish and devoted. Possessed of land,—probably in Cyprus, of which place he was a native —he sold it and gave the whole to the apostles for the use of the infant Christian Church. He was one most ready to recognize the marvellous change in the Apostle Paul, and to take him by the hand. He attested his faith in Paul's sincerity, secured for him the confidence of the apostles. This, however, was not so great a testimony to his charitable and catholic spirit as was his selection by the rest of the apostles to be the deputation to Antioch with respect to a most important church question.

After Christ's ascension, the disciples held to Him as their Saviour, without changing much in

their outward relation to the old form of national worship. They continued to go into the
temple, and to attend to purifications and sacrifices. Only gradually it broke upon them that
Judaism had to be superseded by the religion of
Christ. As regarded those outside Judaism
believing in Christ, the disciples long retained a
prejudice. They could not readily admit them
into the Church, or acknowledge that Christ
could 'profit' them anything, unless they should
first submit to the initiatory rite of Judaism,
and afterwards conform to some of the Mosaic
ceremonies. They believed intensely in their exclusive system. But God shattered their notions.
He allowed persecutions to scatter them abroad.
Though they strove to confine the stream of
heavenly grace within the old limits, it would
find outlet here and there, until at length it broke
down all banks and barriers, and flooded the
world with its fertilizing and gracious riches.

Certain men, fleeing from persecution, travelled to Phenice, Cyprus, and Antioch. In
each place they sought out those who were Jews,
announcing the Gospel to them 'only.' Some
of those who travelled where Jews who had
lived outside Judæa, and had consequently more
liberal views. They ventured to speak of the
wonderful things concerning Christ to the Gentiles. At Antioch they made the most open
declarations, and were so successful, that multitudes believed and found real abiding joy and
peace in Christ.

Tidings of these things reach, either by a special messenger, or by a chance report, the ears of the Christian Church at Jerusalem. Some fear lest this course of action should be opening a door of licence. National exclusiveness is shocked. The Church is in great agitation. This resulted in the appointment of one of their number to go down to Antioch, to see and report upon the new, and to some, strange religious development. But where is the fitting man? Where shall they find one of faithfulness and gentleness, clearness of perception and purity of motive, well-balanced mind and freedom from prejudice? The choice fell upon Barnabas, " a good man, and full of the Holy Ghost and of faith." He went down and recognized the powerful working of God. Like Peter, who went to the house of Cornelius, he dared not, and would not ' withstand God.' When Barnabas " had come and seen the grace of God " he " was glad, and exhorted them all that with purpose of heart they would cleave unto the Lord."

The catholicity of Barnabas may have been fostered by various circumstances. Being a native of Cyprus, although a Jew, and having been brought up away from his own land, he did not so strongly imbibe their national exclusiveness. He had property likewise, and money doubtless enabled him to travel, and come more into contact with his fellow men. This would broaden his mind. He was evidently also a man of some culture. He was a Levite, a pro-

fessed teacher. Like Paul, he may have had
the advantages of a good training. Indeed, it
is possible that they both sat together at the
feet of that great and renowned professor in
Jewish theology and philosophy, Gamaliel.
There they may have met, and learned to
respect each other. This may possibly explain
how it was that Barnabas knew Paul and took
him by the hand, when all the disciples were
afraid of him, testifying to his sincerity and
purity. The qualities he loved and cultivated,
he was most ready to recognize in another.
That he should have so acted in that case indicated how fitted he was to be sent down to
inquire concerning the strange spread of the
doctrine of Christ at Antioch. His gentleness,
and catholicity at this time, and that of Paul
afterwards, probably saved the Gentiles from
forming a sect, distinct from, and hostile to the
Christian Church at Jerusalem.

At Iconium he seems to have kept modestly
in the background, allowing Paul to be the
'chief speaker'; but the Pagans thought doubtless from that majesty and benignity of
countenance that generally accompanies catholicity of spirit that he was Jupiter.

Barnabas was possibly at times led to yield
to an apparent weakness, even through his
charity and catholicity. He was more gentle
and hopeful than Paul concerning John Mark,
who once "departed from them from Pamphylia,
and went not with them to the work" (Acts

xv. 38). His very readiness to believe the best of the erring disciple made the contention between him and Paul so sharp that they 'parted asunder.'

When Jews came down to Antioch and sought to persuade the Jewish Christians in the city to separate themselves from the Gentile Christians, Barnabas seems to have been swayed by their arguments for a time, or to have been actuated by a desire for peace. Paul was pained, and spoke strongly concerning Barnabas being "carried away with the dissimulation" (Gal. ii. 13). He was only 'carried away.' His catholic spirit doubtless soon showed him the error of yielding to the bigoted Jews. Even men of the noblest mind sometimes do things that seem to belie their life. Barnabas was no exception. Where family and national ties were strongly appealed to, Barnabas was led at times to act in a way that must have been quite contrary to his catholicity. His charitableness and peace-loving disposition may even have led to this contradiction.

Distinguish between Catholicism and Catholicity. The one is a pretence, the other is a reality. The former is only a pretence, because it claims to have that which it has not ; but the idea is right. There should be universal submission to Christ, and recognition of all faithful workers in good as having the approval of Christ, and united to Christ. Wherever we find this spirit we call that Christian Catholicity.

It is a belief in the possibility of unity without uniformity. It is something opposed to that spirit which is constantly questioning the Christianity of others. It is a conviction that there may be a oneness of spirit, while diversity of manifestation. It is a longing for reality of spiritual life, rather than reception of narrowing creeds. It is breadth which is the result, not of indifference, but of intelligence; it is a breadth gained by imbibing much of the spirit of Christ.

In reading the life of Christ we find that wherever He could see anything to approve, He did not withhold His approval. He tells one who answered wisely and discreetly, "thou art not far from the kingdom of heaven." He looked upon a young man, who, notwithstanding much self-righteousness, had yet much that was ingenuous, impulsive, and sincere, and "loved" him. He declared the justification of the publican, praised the self-denial of the widow, and the benevolence of the Samaritan. He honoured highly the centurion for his faith, and He pitied the multitudes who had no faith, but were as sheep not having a shepherd. Those for whom He had the most scathing words of rebuke were the men whose duty it was to teach righteousness, and who, when they saw a poor wayfarer lying wounded on the narrow, rocky path, would hurry over to the other side from fear either of life or trouble; or for those who, having murderous intentions in their hearts against Himself, would yet build the tombs of the prophets whom their ancestors slew; or for the self-indulgent Dives, and the indolent, thoughtless steward who hid his talent. Christ thus shows us that while we are to be charitable to all, and show our Catholicity in all things, we may yet cherish a spirit full of holy anger against all evil, against all self-seeking, all self-indulgence, all tyranny, all oppression, and all who morally injure others.

When Jesus sent forth His disciples, He told them to go and do all the good possible. He did not trouble them with any special creed concerning Himself or Divine things. They were to find all the good they might, do all they could, banish all evil, cast out devils, and tread on serpents of error and hate. That is how Christ would have His servants go forth now. Oh, if only we could get that spirit which Christ had, and follow simply His directions, how much uncharitableness would be banished! There would be more effort on the part of good men to come nearer; they would make more allowance for each other's differences of opinion, and denominations would strive to see how they could best lop off anything that was non-essential, and which yet stands in the way of closer union.*

If only we would understand the meaning of the existence of gates on all sides of the New

---

* See Rom. xiv.

Jerusalem, to give entrance from every quarter; we should see that there should be the hope that, although each denomination may be as so many different entrances, they all lead, provided each individual seeks to have the spirit of Christ, to the same blessed end. True Catholicity, also, will lead us to remember that there need not necessarily be but one form of Church life, one ecclesiastical entrance to heaven. God knew our natures and would leave us free to develop individual tendencies. Any one rigid system would be death.

Although by reason of the constitution of our natures, and the various stages of our mental and spiritual growth, there will be differences of opinion and tastes, yet this should not keep us back from the feeling of brotherhood to all who seek in any way to honour God. Every leaf that trembles on the myriad branches of a forest has an individuality of its own, but it helps to make the soft and shadowy glade. Every pebble that lies in the red gravel-pit may have some diversity of form, but it goes to make up the mass. Every wave that tumbles in upon the beach may differ in volume, but it helps to keep up the rhythm of praise to the great Creator. Every star that glitters in the dark blue infinity above us is of varied brilliancy, size, and distance, but they all help to form the constellations, or to compose the nebulæ stretching across the firmament. Thus, in the Christian world, there may be variety of manners, methods of worship or organization, but inasmuch as each holds to Christ and truth, they are filling their appointed sphere, doing their allotted work.

If only we could admit this more readily it would make us more hopeful with respect to the future of the Church. Catholicity is the parent of hopefulness. We are not so ready to think that all who fail to directly associate themselves with us are therefore directly antagonistic. The late good Dean Alford once said, respecting the Church : " It is the more telling mode of speech to distrust, to discredit, to instil alarm and apprehension ; but we confess to have arrived at the more difficult and less popular mode, that of trusting and resting tranquil. The course of history has shown that every step in our advancing series has been more for good, and less for evil, than any of us anticipated; that when we seemed beset with difficulties, and our way hopelessly intricate, the natural conscience struck a clear course, and our apprehended loss became our undeniable gain." Deeply he yearned for true union among Christians, and mourned over strife between them. He saw that the only remedy could be in Christ.

"'One Lord, one faith, one baptism :' where are these ?
'One body and one bread:' I see it not ;
For in the impotence of human thought
Each sinner now himself alone doth please ;
Farewell! sweet love and holy charities ;
Shall it be said that we of God are taught,
While Christian Christian tears, in fierce onslaught

With weapons fetched from carnal armouries?
Therefore, again, Lord God of love, we fall
Before Thy footstool, bold to intercede
For our weak brethren. Hear us, while we plead
For those who Thee forsake, and erring all,
Some of Apollos are, and some of Paul,
In self-directed pride : O Lord, how long?"

At present there is much that seems dark,
hopeless, endless, in the narrowing strife ; but
the truth makes progress. The way may be
broken, curving, and thick with trampled mire,
but it leads to the desired destination. Men
shall one day be more tolerant. They shall see
eye to eye in this at least, that in proportion as
every man is faithful to Christ, apart from all
other questions, he is accepted of Him. The
spirit of Christ is moving over the world, soften-
ing its hardness, and redeeming it from sin. We
look for yet further manifestations of the power
of Christ. Each age shall become more true
and catholic in heart. Christ shall yet gather
together all in one. Let us each seek to advance
the interests of truth, and exercise love towards
our fellows, and so shall we be contributing to
the dawn of that glorious time when the Lord
shall bring again Zion, when the Church shall
no longer hang her head in shame at her
divisions, but lift her heart in praise for the
spiritual unity which has been given. As the
large-hearted, previously-quoted Dean wrote,
out of the fulness of his hopes,

" They tell me
That some have heard the mighty chariot-wheels

18

Roar in the distance ; that the world's salt tears
Are cleaving their last furrows in her cheeks.
It may be so : I know not. Oft the ear,
Attent and eager for some coming friend.
Construes each breeze among the vocal boughs
Into the tokens of his wished approach.
But this I know ; He liveth, and shall stand
Upon this earth ; and round Him, thick as waves
That laugh with light at noon, uncounted hosts
Of His redeemed.
O dawn, millennial day ! Come, blessed morn !
Appear, Desire of nations ! rend Thy heavens,
And stand revealed upon Thy chosen hill !"

We are apt to think that unless lives are run in one special mould, they are not acceptable to God. When we ponder further, we see how varied are the developments and phases they may assume, gaining thereby greater worth. Pattern Christianity, like pattern ornamentation, is generally inferior. Instead of being wrought in stone by slow chisellings, it is moulded in stucco by some rapid process. Reality is thereby lost. Yet in proportion as a man's life is real, pure, natural, and Christ-like, it becomes of golden worth, bears the marks of the Master's strokes, and the secret cypher of the Divine possession. The deeply-graven mark of the Divine Master in the soul of Barnabas was catholicity of spirit.

THE EPHESIAN CHANCELLOR; OR, TUMULT AND OFFICIAL CALM.

SCRIPTURE REFERENCE— *Acts* xix. 35-41.

HEREVER the Gospel was at first preached, opposition was sooner or later surely aroused. The Jew hated its anti-ceremonialistic doctrines, and the Gentile its demand for real purity. At this day men dislike it for similar reasons; first, because it condemns their self-righteousness, and then because it demands consecration of life.

Paul has for two whole years preached at Ephesus the doctrines of the Cross, and with such success, that it seems to have crushed or cowed all opposition. Even those who gained a livelihood by wrong, and by resort to pretended magical arts, give up their evil ways, and, as a proof of their sincerity, bring for destruction two thousand pounds' worth of books, filled with speculations or directions concerning the practice of the "black art." Triumph is on the side of Christ's servants.

"All Asia" not only hears the truth but is amazed at its power.

Now comes trouble. Rosy dawn is changed to thunderous gloom. Opposition to the Gospel is raised by those who have vested interests in wrong. The spread of Christianity interferes with the shrine-making trade. The demand for the little silver images of Diana, for coins with her superscription, for models of her temple, for various mementoes of her special worship, grows less and less. The shrine-makers meet one another, and confess that they never knew business so dull. Where they formerly sold ten shrines to the residents or pilgrims, now they cannot sell one. They know they are engaged in a farce, but then the sham brings profit and pelf to their coffers. This check to trade must be enquired into. Demetrius gets together a council of trade and of war. The various members of that council acknowledge that Christ's truth is demolishing Diana-worship. They have capital invested in that worship. If false, it must be sustained for the sake of such capitalists. Their interest and per-centages they must have. Moreover, the artizans who work for the capitalists are annoyed and alarmed also. Capital and labour at Ephesus combined against Christ. Both find a spokesman in Demetrius. His frank utterance is, "Our craft is in danger." He makes his appeal simply to self-interest. This was the moving power. To give it leverage he added a pretended zeal for the religion of the city. Those who wished to be monetary gainers might become so under hypocritical pretence of devotion. Anyhow, a great hubbub was soon raised. Mobs gather. Staid citizens are alarmed. There is much hurrying and concentrating of crowds. They mutually foster bitterness. Increasing masses mutter curses, deep and daring. " They were filled with wrath, and for the space of two hours cried out, ' Great is Diana of the Ephesians.' The whole city was filled with confusion." Two of Paul's fellow-travellers were caught and hustled into the public hall. Here the shouting goes on still. The heated crowd will listen to no one. It is not reason or argument they want, but concession. The con- cession demanded is the suppression of the liberty of Gospel preaching. Paul's teaching must be stopped. If his heart could cease to beat, as well as his mouth be shut, they would be content. If he can meet with his death through this uproar, the movers of the tumult will not complain. Demetrius, like a true coward, sneaks away from the forefront of the excited mob ; and we can hear him whispering to himself,

> " Mischief, thou art afoot ;
> Now let it work."

He takes care to get out of harm's way ; but if murder should result, and the noble Paul or any of the disciples should chance to meet with crippling or crushing violence, he will try to soothe his conscience by the thought that, although the prompter of the murder, he had not been the actual perpetrator. He only gave a signal, but did not drive home the knife. The tumultuous crowd were his stupid dupes. They may do the mean work, he will reap the golden results. Vested interests aroused the bitter opposition to the Gospel.

The tumult at Ephesus was only a *type of that opposition which still goes on against the Gospel.* The truth of Christ still agitates the minds of men. They talk about it, discuss it, preach about it, write about it. Some love it, others faintly praise it ; while others ignore, denounce, undermine, deny, oppose, and blaspheme it. Many wish the Gospel were quietly shelved or perhaps decently buried. They pretend that the religion of Christ is only an old-time superstition that has troubled the world long enough. It will remain in the world longer. It must live. It must go on rebuking sin and lifting up the sinful. It comes from God. It tells of His love. It provides a way of release from sin, and hope for souls. It fosters purity and produces love ; yet men oppose it. Why ? Men find it easier to yield to evil, to passion, greed, lust, selfishness, and worldliness, than to harmonize life with its requirements. Sin will create a disturbance rather than be dismissed from the heart. In the world also it is seen to foster much uproar and outcry. We have had evidence enough of this of late. The wild shrieking of atheistic blasphemy and the whisperings of self-satisfied speculators in science, are all indications of the fact that Christianity is alive and a power. Christ said, " I came not to send peace, but a sword." That sword of truth must be wielded with slashing power and deadly swoop, until error shall be slain and sin put to flight.

The opposition raised in Ephesus was not only a type of the opposition to the gospel, but also of its *unreasoning character*. If men were unprejudiced, they could not but see how beneficial are the effects of Christianity. What else has softened suffering, reared hospitals, elevated woman, tended the orphan, opened prison cells, struck off fetters from the slave, cheered the despairing, thrown a bright light into the gloomy grave, revealed an actual state of bliss and immortality beyond the tomb? What else makes man to-day look with tenderness, and yet hopefulness, on the toiling, struggling, forlorn masses of all lands? The benefits of Christianity cannot be denied, and yet there are those who look upon it with despite and even hate. Many are trying to create such a state of feeling against it, as Demetrius created when he stirred up the silver-workers to make that two-hours' tumult in Ephesus. There are many, however, who know not why they are opposed. They are like those " who knew not wherefore they were come together." They know not definitely what they object to in the

Bible or Christ, but they are content to stand aloof, or mingle with the tumultuous opponents in unreasoning opposition.

Now look at the clever *way in which the tumult was quelled.* The Chancellor, Recorder, or Town Clerk, made his way boldly into the assembly and stationed himself where he could command the whole seething mass. Soon every eye was fixed on him, and every ear attent to catch his words, Whether awe of his official authority or desire to have his favour acted on them, they listened to his utterances. They may have expected him to take sides with them against the disciples. As the Roman guardian of the temple, surely he was concerned for the worship of Diana, therefore they listened ; gaining their ears he soon gains their assent.

First he shows that there is *no need for uproar.* He pretends that Diana's worship is too firmly established to be overthrown. He seeks to win, not to drive. Opposition is dissipated by a firm gentleness. He knew well that a " lion may be stroked into bondage when he would not be beaten into a chain." He knew that soft words turn away wrath, just as the sun, in the fable, was more successful than the wind in removing the traveller's cloak.

The Chancellor knew how to persuade by *establishing a sense of the unity of interests* between himself and the agitated. Whatever slight fell on the temple fell on him. So in meeting the opponents of the truth, we who are

preachers or private Christians may say. " We
have as much at stake as you, and are not
anxious to be deceived. Indeed, we have more
to risk, for if there be no truth in that which
we believe Christ has revealed, we are " of all
men most miserable."

The Chancellor knew, further, that to *assert
a conviction* was the best way to check the
spread of opposition. He saw that the disciples
were " not robbers of churches," and he said so.
He looked at them honestly. He judged by
their works. He judged not by the weak and
inconsistent, but by the strong. The world
ofttimes delights to act in a contrary manner,
and seeks to damage religion by pointing to the
weak and faulty, while it lets the stately host
of the true and pure pass on unnoticed, unap-
proved and unapplauded. This Roman Chancellor stood up and, single-handed, opposed a
false representation. He did that although he
knew that he was taking an unpopular course.
The man was like a rock, standing unmoved by
the waters of the foaming torrent. What a
lesson in courage for the wavering and faint-
hearted !

The Chancellor showed the *power of individual action.* What *one* man can do ! Men
generally like to go in droves, like sheep ;
here was one who could stand against a crowd,
a world. One man " chased a thousand and put
ten thousand to flight."

A lesson was distinctly taught by this Roman

official concerning the *danger of rash action*, and of resort to unlawful expedients. He saw through the pretended zeal of Demetrius, and rebuked it. Lawful measures, not illegal, rash measures, he recommended. The Forum was open, counsel was to be had for payment. Let there be fair judging. Mere tumult cannot silence truth. Boldness is a virtue, rashness a vice. We ought always to be zealous in a good cause, but " we ought to do nothing rashly," for rashness and wrong are often closely allied.

The *importance of acting in the present with a view to the future* was insisted upon by the Ephesian town clerk. " We are in danger to be called in question for this day's uproar." As a Roman magistrate, he might not tolerate anything riotous. Tidings of any such thing reaching headquarters would imperil his position. He knew that there was nothing to justify the day's doings,—" no cause whereby we may give account of this day's concourse." As men, we should keep the future judgment before us, remembering that we, too, have to give an account.

But in all the Chancellor's words and actions, we see that he was not acting under any strong conviction of the truth of Christianity. He was *calm and firm because not greatly concerned.* He was anxious only for the preservation of peace. Indifference can afford to be calm ; but when we feel strongly, we are then likely to act with impetuosity. The indifferent would condemn the over-enthusiasm of some Christians; but if they felt the power of the truth as others feel it, they would not sit down so calmly, or glide along so easily. Calmness and indifference never stir the world. While taking what is good in the advice of the town clerk, let us not imbibe his spirit of indifference. He was an official representing the liberal spirit of the empire that tolerated all religions, because it had no deep faith in any.

We need to be in earnest, to remember the account we have to give of the life lent. The present state of Ephesus is a type of what will be the final state of a soul or Church that lacks spiritual earnestness. The waters have receded from the city. Its once busy wharves are now silent. Its water-way is silted up. No gay galley longer rows in front of its temple and palaces. The place, once a centre of Asian wealth and commerce, is now a heap of desolate ruins. Under its broken archways we wandered, and over its masses of fallen marbles and masonry; and everywhere in the city and on the treeless, bare neighbourhood, seemed written in living characters the one word, " Forsaken." That will be written on the soul if we know not the time of our visitation, and if we act not with decision for Christ. Let not then the calmness of indifference characterize us. As with ease the Chancellor dismissed the assembly, let us not dismiss these thoughts. If we think Christianity untrue, we should see to it that we have very satisfactory grounds for coming to so terrible a conclusion. If untrue, we would join the mob of Demetrius, and, heedless of the counsel of the Ephesian Chancellor, would think only of our craft, our temporal interests, and how, by mobs and schemings and shoutings, to secure their preservation. But we are sure that Christianity is from God, for it could not otherwise have survived the misrepresentations of its professed friends or the bitter hate of its opponents. If from God, it demands the devotion of our heart and the consecration of our life.

1868.53   J. WRIGHT & Co., Printers, Bristol.